Guarding the Air

Guarding the Air

Selected Poems of Gunnar Harding

Translated and edited by Roger Greenwald

BLACK WIDOW PRESS

BOSTON, MA

The cost of this translation was defrayed by a subsidy from the Swedish Arts Council, gratefully acknowledged. The publisher also thanks the Barbro Osher Pro Suecia Foundation for its generous support. RG thanks Glenna Munro for expert advice.

Some of these translations were published from 1989 to 2009 in *WRIT Magazine, Stand Magazine, Samizdat, Manhattan Review, ICE-FLOE, Journal of Literature and Aesthetics, Leviathan Quarterly, Two Lines, The Kenyon Review, ARS-INTERPRES, Fourteen Hills, Typo, Words without Borders, Lyric*, and *SALT*.

www.blackwidowpress.com
Joseph S. Phillips and Susan J. Wood, PhD, Publishers

Cover art: Roger de la Fresnaye, *La conquête de l'air* (1913)
Author photo: Paula Tranströmer. Used by permission.

ISBN-13: 978-0-9856122-7-6
Printed in the United States

10 9 8 7 6 5 4 3 2 1

These translations are dedicated to
Stephen Kessler and Daniela Hurezanu

CONTENTS

from *Parlor Music* (2001)

from *The Burning Child* (2003)

INTRODUCTION

Gunnar Harding (born 1940) is one of Sweden's foremost poets, and also one of its best liked. He started as a jazz musician, studied painting in Stockholm, and made his literary debut in 1967. He has published—in addition to translations and non-fiction—seventeen volumes of poetry (including his prose poetry), most recently *Det Brinnande barnet* (The Burning Child) in 2003. In 1992 he was awarded the Bellman Prize by the Swedish Academy. 1993 saw publication of a comprehensive selection of his poetry under the title *Överallt där vinden finns: Dikter i urval 1969–1990* (Wherever the Wind Is Blowing: Selected Poems 1969–1990). In 1995 he was awarded *Svenska Dagbladets* Literature Prize in recognition of his important role in Sweden's literary life since the 1960s, and in 2001 he won the prestigious Övralid Prize.

Brief mention of some of Harding's work aside from poetry will suggest the breadth of his career. His non-fiction includes a collection of essays and articles covering the period 1971–77, and *Kreol* (Creole), a book about the roots of jazz. He has translated numerous writers into Swedish, for example Apollinaire, Cendrars, Khlebnikov, Mayakovsky, Ginsberg, Charles Olson, Keats, and Shelley. He has also edited several anthologies: in 1979, *Modern Swedish Poetry in Translation* (with Anselm Hollo), in 1995, *Är vi långt från Montmartre: Apollinaire och hans epok i poesi, bild och dokument* (Are We Far from Montmartre: Apollinaire and His Epoch in Poetry, Picture and Document), and in 1997, *En katedral av färgat glas: Shelley, Byron, Keats och deras epok* (A Dome of Many-coloured Glass: Shelley, Byron, Keats and Their Epoch), a collection and presentation of English Romantic poetry in Swedish translation. Harding served on Sweden's Bible Commission, with the responsibility of ensuring that the new Bible translation then under preparation would retain adequate poetic force. Starting in the 1970s, he edited the magazine *Lyrikvännen* (The Poetry-lover); for many years he was co-editor of the Swedish literary quarterly *ARTES;* and for its five-year run, he was co-editor of the English-language annual *ARTES INTERNATIONAL.*

In his youth, Harding spent extended periods in the U.S.; those visits, along with his background in painting and his lifelong devotion to jazz, have had a noticeable influence on his work. Harding's poetry is both accessible and appealing, marked by a strong intellect and a great gift for imagery. Anselm Hollo wrote that the poems are informed by "a consistently lively balance and tension between vividly visual information and the seemingly effortless musical structure that contains and carries the information."[1] Above all, this is poetry with heart; it is unsentimental, but also unafraid to address a wide range of emotions that most readers will recognize.

Harding himself has written a brief but useful guide to his poetry in the form of the prefaces to his three volumes of selected poems; English versions of these follow this introduction (the first preface is here slightly abridged). I will therefore refrain from further critical comment and will turn instead to a few remarks about the present book.

My aim in choosing the poems for this book has been to present a fairly comprehensive selection of Gunnar Harding's best poetry. The poet gave me his views on the selection but kindly left the final choice to me. I asked of each poem that it be excellent and that it be able to "travel" into English. In spite of applying such stringent criteria, however, I found that the manuscript would be quite large. Partly to make its length manageable and partly to ensure the coherence of the book, Harding and I agreed on certain exclusions: I would include only verse, and I would not make selections from one book that we both felt should be presented in its entirety or not at all.

This meant that Harding's first book would be unrepresented here, since the only poems from it I had intended to include—and the only ones Harding now cares to see in print—are prose poems. It also meant leaving out the two books of wonderful prose poems on Apollinaire, as well as one book of poems in verse, *Starnberger See* (Lake Starnberg), from 1977. Part of the first book on Apollinaire, *Guillaume Apollinaires fantastiska liv* (1971), has been published in English: *The Fabulous Life of Guillaume Apollinaire,* trans. Sydney Bernard Smith (Iowa City: Windhover, 1970 and Dublin: Raven Arts, 1982); and the whole book, with additions and revisions at each publication, has appeared in several languages, including French: *Le fabuleuse existence de Guillaume Apollinaire,* trans. Jacques Outin (Castelnau-le-Lez: Climats, 1990). As for *Starnberger See,* Robin Fulton has translated selections from it (London: Oasis, 1983; out of print). Fulton has also translated a selection of twenty-five early poems by Harding, published in 1973 as *They Killed Sitting Bull and other poems*

1. *Modern Swedish Poetry in Translation* (Minneapolis: University of Minnesota Press, 1979), 109.

(London Magazine Editions, out of print). Most of the translations in that selection have been reprinted, together with a few additional translations by Anselm Hollo, in *Tidewater* (Grosse Pointe Farms, MI: Marick Press, 2009).

My translations have as usual gone through many stages of revision over the course of several years. Gunnar Harding's help has been invaluable, not only because of the insight he has given me into his poems, but because as an experienced translator he has always understood the process sympathetically, from the inside out. He has responded in his good-natured way to countless written questions, and has gone over drafts with me in Toronto and Stockholm and Visby, always managing to inject humor into a potentially tedious traversal of detail. I am also especially grateful to my fellow poet Richard Lush, who has read my English versions closely and given me the benefit of his perceptive criticisms and suggestions. I should mention that English translations of three of the poems in this selection appear in *Modern Swedish Poetry in Translation*. I probably read those translations years ago, but I did not revisit them until my own translations were in near-final form. And I did not read Robin Fulton's translations until I was preparing the data files for the present book.

Lena Pasternak and Gerda Helena Lindskog provided a warm welcome and excellent facilities at the Baltic Centre for Writers and Translators in Visby. The Swedish Institute and its staff, especially Helen Sigeland and Elisabeth Seth, made my work easier and my stays in Stockholm fruitful. Many years ago, Elisabeth Hall, who then worked at the Institute, first put a book of Gunnar Harding's poems in my hands; it was *Tillbaka till dig* (Back to You), so perhaps it is appropriate to conclude the long process of creating this book by returning to its starting point and thanking her for that happy gift.

Roger Greenwald
2013

AUTHOR'S PREFACES

Poesi 1967–1973 (Poetry 1967–1973)

What have I done? What have I done? That's what the pope cries out, horrified, near the beginning of my counterfeit biography of Apollinaire. I made the same exclamation in the same tone more than once as I was going through my earlier collections of poems in order to put together this selection. Some pages have yellowed; others seem to have been written by a person completely unknown to me. On many pages, however, I recognize myself: my weaknesses but also, I'm happy to say, my qualities.

Certain typical characteristics of my poems have to do with my special "cultural background." From 1955 to 1960 I was an enthusiastic—more than exactly successful—member of several traditional jazz bands. I've never pursued any clear "jazz tone" in my poems, but I think that especially in the earlier ones, different themes are interwoven in a way that resembles the interplay of the different instruments in a New Orleans jazz band. I suppose one can also discover in them both "breaks" and foot-stamping. Traditional jazz developed in parallel with the 78-rpm record, which lent it obvious "poetic" qualities. Recording forced the musicians to blow out as much as they could in under three minutes. After that it was too late. So this jazz form, like poetry, was highly charged with energy and limited in time. My enthusiasm for Bix Beiderbecke hasn't diminished with the years, but rather has been complemented by an interest in such composers as Satie, Charles Ives, and Stravinsky. They too have probably left traces in the poems.

Painting has also meant a great deal to me. At one time that was really what I wanted to devote myself to. I still envy painters that smell of turpentine and linseed oil, and the feeling you get when you squeeze long paint-snakes out of the tubes and daub them onto the canvas. That way of working was more alive than rattling out dead letters on a machine.

It is self-evident that I write in a tradition that is sooner visual than analytic…. One of my severest critics wrote that I consider imagination superior to reality. This is not true…. I try, with the help of imagination, to portray a part of reality, and with that same denigrated imagination perhaps also to create a reality. In my way of writing poetry, in general I want imagination, reason, feelings and knowledge to work in synch to produce high pressure…. It is the literary researcher's task to dig up the truth behind the myths. One of the poet's tasks is to keep the myths alive and invent new ones. There is no contradiction between "myth" and "reality." They are both parts of Reality.

Flowers for James Dean (1969)

America. I belong to the generation that watched as America conquered Sweden bit by bit, the generation that was itself conquered by America. I was five years old when the Second World War ended and the newsstand at the streetcar terminal for line 13 filled up with bubblegum and comics. With drawn sword Errol Flynn took the movie matinées by storm as Robin Hood, as General Custer, as Captain Blood. Pocketknives carved the mark of Zorro on the pine trees in the Ulvsunda woods. Then came the first jeans, and then Coca-Cola. It was impossible to resist. Sport-cola, Master Detective Blomkvist, plus fours and Loranga—all of domestic culture began to teeter.

Then came jazz. But with it, something else too. *Strange fruit hangin' from the poplar trees,* Billie Holiday sang. In the basement clubs of the Old Town, a short, sentimental poem by Langston Hughes circulated in pencil copies: *Way Down South in Dixie / (Break the heart of me) / They hung my black young lover / To a cross roads tree.*[2] That led me toward American literature. Richard Wright's novels of segregation and race-hatred in the South. Carl Sandburg: *They tell me you are wicked and I believe them.*[3] Then the shots in Dallas. The murders of Malcolm X and Martin Luther King. The Lyndon Johnson era. And year after year, the war in Vietnam. *With a sudden smell of burnin' flesh,* Billie Holiday sang.[4]

I came to the USA in September, 1968, only a short time after the demonstrators at the Democratic Convention in Chicago had been met with tear gas and police batons. It was the year of revolt, but also the year Nixon was elected, a year when pessimism and gloom spread among radicals in the US.

---

2. "Song for a Dark Girl," first published in *Saturday Review of Literature* (19 April 1927), 712, and in *Crisis* (May 1927), 94. Collected in *Fine Clothes to the Jew* (New York: Knopf, 1927). See *The Collected Poems of Langston Hughes,* ed. Arnold Rampersand (New York: Knopf, 1994), 104, 626. I have supplied all the notes to these prefaces, except note 11. —RG

3. "Chicago," Sandburg's first published poem, which appeared in *Poetry* in 1914.

4. "Strange Fruit," by Lewis Allen. E. B. Marks Music (BMI).

Flowers for James Dean. The title is an echo of the American anarchist song "Give flowers to the rebels failed." The time was past for private rebellion, the individualist revolt portrayed by James Dean in the film *Rebel without a Cause.* (The film ended, moreover, with the boy introducing his girl to his parents, and—one can infer—with his comforming to society's norms.) Behind the failed rebels there rose up the image of Che Guevara.

On the Indian reservation in Tama, Iowa, I saw the remaining fragments of another American people, another American lifestyle. When the US Army crushed Crazy Horse and Sitting Bull, they crushed that people who first dreamed the great American dream of living free in a vast land. Paradoxically enough, it was the same dream that official America was still battling in tear-gassed Chicago, in Southeast Asia, in South America. Over and over, American imperialism leads to new Wounded Knee's, new Song My's; over and over it kills as well what is central to an American radical tradition.

But during the year when I lived in the US, I also met something else: people who thought as I did, who lived as I did, who read the same books, who were working to create a living poetry that would involve the whole person—the whole mind, all organs; dreams and thoughts, reason and feelings.

All this happened so fast. And I wrote fast. Images, myths and real events spiraled around one another and resulted in the volume of poems *Flowers for James Dean.*

The Eagle Has Landed (1970)

On 20 July 1969 the Apollo Project achieved its goal when the lunar lander *The Eagle* touched down on the moon. I received the news while lying in the bathtub. Until then I had connected July 20th with an entirely different event—the assassination attempt against Hitler on 20 July 1944, when Count Stauffenberg planted a bomb that exploded in Hitler's headquarters. Not knowing that Hitler had survived the explosion, Stauffenberg set in motion Operation Valkyrie, under which anti-Nazis would try to seize power. The attempted coup had tragic consequences: a large part of the German resistance movement revealed itself and could therefore be neutralized by bloody purges. From a film about the July 20th coup I remember a scene in which the conspiring officers, when they believe that Hitler has been eliminated, rip the Nazi eagles from their uniforms. Twenty-five years later *The Eagle* lands on the moon and Richard Nixon, proud and moved, talks to the crew on the telephone...

In *The Eagle Has Landed* I took up some of the same themes as in *Flowers for James Dean*. On the other hand, I abandoned the technique of concretizing contemporary problems in the guise of film stars, Indian chiefs and historical figures. In this book I retained, however, the use of montage, as I have done in my writing since then. That history and personal memories exist in the present dimension, that "reality" consists of both outer and inner experiences that collide, break against each other, are colored by each other, that a multitude of actions occur *simultaneously*—all this is organically incorporated in my way of apprehending the world. To invent "typical" people, put them in "typical" situations, and relate that first this happened and then that happened and then he went home—that is often called realism. What it is, in fact, is "literature"—and as Breton pointed out, literature is the opposite of poetry.

Search Line (1972)

I have spent a good deal of my life traveling. I love to travel in all four directions and preferably a few more. Movement has always interested me. I can see this even in the drawings I made at the age of four. The person who once made those drawings was certainly interested in how people and things appeared, but above all he was interested in how they moved—especially if they moved fast. Not very strange, then, that two decades later he was a pushover for what Charles Olson wrote: "get on with it, keep moving, keep in, speed, the nerves, their speed, the perceptions, theirs, the acts, the split second acts, the whole business, keep it moving as fast as you can, citizen. And if you also set up as a poet, USE USE USE the process at all points, in any given poem always, always one perception must must must MOVE, INSTANTER, ON ANOTHER!"[5]

Traveling at high speed has its advantages. You get to see a whole lot. But it also has its drawbacks. Often you get to observe things for only a short time. You don't ever really get to put down roots somewhere. In *Search Line* I began to dig in search of my own roots in my native country and my local milieu. I also sat down and started digging in myself. Between this book and the preceding ones there also lay an ongoing reading of Jung.

5. From Olson's well-known essay, "Projective Verse," in *Poetry New York* (No. 3, 1950), and reprinted in *The New American Poetry*, ed. Donald M. Allen (New York: Grove, 1960).

Cape Farewell (1973)

The poem "Cape Farewell" isn't yet part of any of my volumes of poetry, but since it contains something of a poetic "program," I've included it as the last poem in this selection.

That one of Harry Martinson's best-known books (which I haven't read) has the same title never occurred to me when I wrote the poem, and I have therefore let the title stand.[6]

To find reality beyond the maps of it, beyond what we know, under language but also with the help of language. Words often deceive. What does a designation like "King Christian ix Land" say about the place it is supposed to describe? Was he ever there? To write poetry is to be there, to be *here* to as high a degree as possible. And thus everything I quoted from Charles Olson: get on with it, keep moving…

Överallt där vinden finns: Dikter i urval 1969–1990 (Wherever the Wind Is Blowing: Selected Poems)

Having published, in the course of twenty-five years, enough books to make an overview difficult, I have seen myself and my poems described a great many times by knowledgeable and insightful people. What remains to be said? Perhaps just that I can't recall that any of these descriptions has moved me to exclaim: That's me! That's what my poetry is like!

Now that I myself have the opportunity to describe my poetry, I nevertheless find myself stuck. It's just as annoying to be hemmed in by yourself as by others—perhaps because one of the compelling motives behind the act of writing is to take yourself outside the realm of the defined. The poem isn't necessarily a summing up; it can also be a growing, a breaking out.

When you've devoted yourself for decades to writing down your imaginings, it's easy to find in them certain patterns that recur. Many advances into new ground, as I once thought of them, were in fact only reprises. A person who expresses his thoughts only in speech can easily convince himself and others that he is a person of rich imagination, since neither he nor his listeners remember what he said fifteen years earlier. But when you put together a collection of writing, you can't count on any such merciful forgetfulness.

6. Harry Martinson (1904–1978) was awarded the Nobel Prize for Literature in 1974. *Kap Farväl!* (Cape Farewell!), a book of prose pieces based on Martinson's youthful experiences as a sailor, was published in 1933.

Naturally there are some poems that I can identify with more easily than I can with others. Here and there I discover lines that are absolutely written by me. This doesn't necessarily imply that they're the best ones I've written, just that I've caught in them a glimpse of something that I grasp as myself, as for example in the poem "My Winterland":

Fanns där en snubblande barmhärtighet,
tumvantar i lådor, tafatta famntag mellan anförvanter
som bara kan övervinnas genom att beskrivas?
På detta sätt kan stenen förflyttas, lämna en gata i snön
liknande de stråk av gräs som uppstår vid uppförandet
av snögubbar. Stenkolsögon. Grus till tänder,
obegripligt efter snösmältningen.
Inte ens experter kan skilja det vatten
som en gång varit snö från vanligt vatten.

Was there a bumbling mercy,
knitted mittens in drawers, relatives trading stiff embraces
which one can only overcome by describing them?
In this way the stone can be moved, can leave a lane in the snow
like the runners of grass left rolled out when you build
snowmen. Charcoal eyes. Gravel for teeth,
indiscernible after the snow has melted.
Not even experts can distinguish water
that once was snow from ordinary water.

I have to confess that after the fact I revel in the loopy alliteration "tum-vantar," "tafatta famntag," "anförvanter"—in all its fuzzy lack of contact. And as far as I know, no other poet has documented the runners of grass that appear in the snow where someone has rolled a snowball; nor has any-one asked which bits of gravel and charcoal belonged to a snowman before the thaw. In hindsight I appreciate too how the poet, just when he's made this discovery, dissolves the whole thing in the absent-minded offhand comment about the experts on melted snow.

An author is undeniably a somewhat special reader of his own poems. Often I read straight through them, see the locales, events and feelings that gave rise to them. I know which awkward hugs the poem refers to. I could even point out the exact spot where the snowman stood. But I do not doubt that the reader can fill out the poems with his own hugs and snowmen.

Other poems refer in a more general way to shared experiences, to what is usually called "our situation." In such poems of the times it is possible that my poetic method complicates the reading process. I'm not at all sure that everyone will perceive, for example, that the poem "The Night Wanderer" portrays in great detail the first trial of Christer Pettersson, who at that point still had no face and no name in the media.[7] The newspapers printed a black blot over his face; radio and TV bleeped out his name. The title alludes to the statement by one of Palme's sons that the man he had seen outside the Grand cinema reminded him of the painting *The Night Wanderer*, a work of art I wasn't able to identify.[8] I wrote the poem during my lunchtime walks in Kungsträdgården,[9] with questions and answers from the trial echoing in my mind: the prosecutor's quotation from the Book of Job about the righteous man who, though blameless, must suffer affliction;[10] Christer Pettersson's claim that he had "a built-in clock." But does the reader see this poem as anything other than a confusing pile of images?

The source of such problems may be that I have never really tried to describe surface reality as such, but rather how impressions from it collide in my consciousness and are colored there by memories and associations. To try to capture the present as it rushes by is a hopeless task. Before the pen has managed to fix it to the page, it has already changed—if one sees the present as something outside oneself that whirls by in a flash. But if we see the poetic present as something that exists in our own consciousness, it can be extended in all directions via chains of associations. Then the poem does not

7. In December 1989, Christer Pettersson was charged with having assassinated Olof Palme, Prime Minister of Sweden, on 28 February 1986. At his first trial he was convicted, but the conviction was quashed on appeal, on the grounds that the evidence did not prove guilt beyond a reasonable doubt. In December 1997, the prosecutor's office applied to the Supreme Court of Sweden for permission to try Pettersson again on the basis of new evidence. In 1998 the Court denied such permission.

8. Most likely a late (1939) self-portrait by Edvard Munch (1963–1944), also known as *Peer Gynt*. See the endnote on this poem.

9. The King's Garden, a famous, tradition-rich park in downtown Stockholm. It is a heavily used open area with statuary, fountains, paths, benches, and various entertainments (such as large-scale chess games). Greenery consists of shrubs within the park and trees along its edges, where outdoor cafés and merchants' stalls have made notable inroads.

10. The prosecutor was referring to the way Pettersen described himself.

become thoughts set in verse or clothed in metaphors. It becomes "the poet's way of thinking," a representation of the very process of consciousness.

I've never tried to hide which poets have influenced me. They are the ones I translated and presented to Swedish readers. But then, I have never seen delving into other poets' work as a threat to my independence.

In Swedish the word *original* has come to denote something singular, almost eccentric. It's almost as if we forget that the word's real meaning is "primary, primordial." That the word has been distorted in our language is a sure sign that people have chosen to marginalize the most central concept in it.

It's said that we're born originals but we die as copies. Whoever coined this saying seems to have regarded the word *original* as a positive one, which suggests the author was a foreign thinker. And sure enough, he turns out to have been the eighteenth-century English orator Edward Young.

But the saying also seems to have it that originality is something static. Naturally this isn't true, whether in literary or other human contexts. Our speech is born in conversation. With people we trust, we talk in a more personal way. At the same time as our voice is colored by the other person's, in such a conversation we also become more ourselves. That's how literary influences work too. Voices we care about give power, breadth and stimulation to our own, and bring out new qualities. We develop into originals, in constant communication with people who have something to teach us about ourselves.

As a writer of poetry I am usually labeled an enthusiastic modernist, and as a writer on jazz, a hopeless traditionalist and anti-modernist. The complete incompatibility of the two labels has probably arisen because few people have familiarized themselves with both parts of my work. If I look back over what I have written about poetry through the years, I find that it has often been attacks on people who chose to limit poetry to *one* form of poem. Naturally there is no basic rule for what good poetry should look like or sound like. No single poetic direction has a monopoly on brilliance.

If I look at which traditions have influenced me most deeply, I find they have in common that they join spontaneous improvisation with knowledge of the traditions. To set up tradition and renewal as opposed concepts in the first place is totally foreign to me. There is a great deal that's new that we must assimilate so as not to stagnate, but there is also a great deal we must hold on to so as not to lose ourselves.

I don't think I have ever called myself a modernist. I would prefer not to see myself circumscribed by a system. Nor do I think it is fruitful to adhere to a movement that includes such incompatible phenomena as the buildings in Hötorgscity[11] and the poems of André Breton. I would prefer to describe myself as a person with a varied range of possibilities that are not necessarily determined by loyalty to a certain system of thought or a certain direction in art. But perhaps it is precisely this attitude that is meant by "modernism."

In recent years I have, however, discovered certain advantages in being always associated with a lost cause. When Rhett Butler leads Scarlett O'Hara out of the burning city of Atlanta in *Gone with the Wind,* they cross the path of the scattered remnants of the Confederate Army. Rhett, taking leave of Scarlett, says that he's thinking now of joining the crushed army. During their victorious years he had remained skeptical toward "the great cause." Even though I don't consider the ideas of the Confederacy worth fighting for, I find this attitude appealing. Whoever allies himself with a lost cause avoids joining up with opportunists, fellow-travelers, and profiteers. Those are always on the other side.

I've never been ashamed of the visual qualities in my poetry, even though they have never been in fashion during the whole time I've been writing. Because at a certain time in my youth I took the step over to poetry from painting, I have always regarded the poetic image as central. Anyone who studies the cultural journalism of the past few decades can't avoid the impression that these years constituted a period of decline for visual poetry. Anyone who goes instead to the poems themselves soon finds that the same epoch—from Tranströmer's *Den halvfärdiga himlen* (The Half-built Heaven) in 1962 to Bruno Öijer's *Medan giftet verkar* (While the Poison Works) in 1990—can just as well be described as the time when metaphorical poetry attained perfection.

A visual language evokes suspicion in our puritanical culture. It's the language of dreams, a language of the unconscious, above all a seductive language. Practitioners of the New Simplicity, Marxists, and postmodernists alike have dismissed it as the language of modernism. This is correct insofar as the disappearance of end-rhyme from poetry gave metaphor a

11. During the 1950s a large part of central Stockholm was torn down and rebuilt in quite a boring modern style, with halfhearted skyscrapers at Hötorgscity. Many historically interesting old buildings were wiped out to make way for car-parks and banks. Hötorgscity is like a symbol of this, the destruction of one of the few European capitals that came out of World War II intact. —G.H.

more dominant role. Metaphor too makes a sort of rhyme, but not one built on like sounds, as is end-rhyme, which has forever coupled concepts like "ljus" and "grus" (light and gravel), "konung" and "honung" (king and honey). Metaphor yields increased possibilities for establishing deeper and more surprising connections—or disconnects, if that's what you want.

But the technique is of course far from new: Aristotle in his *Poetics* maintained that the foremost poets were those who were masterly in their use of metaphor, "[f]or this alone cannot be gained from others and is a sign of the naturally well-endowed poet."[12]

It is a widespread misconception that the visual poet translates "visions" into poems. It's sooner a question of creating images, visions, illuminations in language. To praise the absence of this ability in a poet seems to me about as carefully considered as applauding a person because he has scurvy or beriberi.

English Romantic poetry has always meant a great deal to me. In recent years my interest has shifted from Shelley's revolutionary idealism and Blake's mysterious visions to Keats's odes and his defense of the poet's "negative capability," that is, the capability of "being in uncertainties, mysteries, doubts, without any irritable reaching after fact and reason."[13] Rarely has this capacity been so necessary as in recent years, when so many certainties have withered into doubts.

In these inflationary times, it also becomes steadily more difficult to formulate cocksure assertions about poetry, or in poetry. The basis for writing is no longer knowledge about what is happening, but sooner knowledge about not knowing. But uncertainty too can be a poetic method: to try to find your way from something you merely sense to something you don't yet understand.

It's not always so easy to maintain the faith that this activity is meaningful. Something more than uncertainty is required.

Keats put it this way: "I am certain of nothing but of the holiness of the Heart's affections, and the truth of Imagination." He continued: "What the imagination seizes as Beauty must be truth—whether it existed before or not."[14]

The slightly Romantic language can make it difficult to discern anything living and of current relevance in what Keats says. Words like *truth* and

12. Aristotle *Poetics* 22.1459a, trans. Kenneth A. Telford (Chicago: Regnery, 1961).
13. Letter to George and Thomas Keats, undated, probably 21 December 1817.
14. Letter to Benjamin Bailey, 22 November 1817.

beauty can now be understood almost exclusively in the plural. They've been multiplied. I know it sounds sentimental, but I believe it is important to keep faith in this truth of the imagination. Moreover—even though it sounds still more sentimental—I believe that it is important to insist that the feelings that come from the heart are sacred. If they are missing, then we are facing a devaluation not only of truth and beauty, but also of poetry.

Dikter 1965–2003 (Poems 1965–2003)

"I'm standing in Ulvsunda Place / with my hands in my pockets / whistling 'St. Louis Blues' off-key." That's how the first poem in this volume of selected work begins, and that's how I must have perceived myself as I began my poetic career. Or rather, that's how I wanted to be perceived. This poem was written before the poems in my first book. I regard it as my first poem, despite the fact that before writing it I had written a good deal of poetry that magazines and publishing houses, fortunately, had rejected. But in this poem I felt I had written my way up to "the point that initiates meaning." This isn't to say that the poem is strikingly able to stand on its own. It resonates throughout with the influence of the San Francisco poet Lawrence Ferlinghetti. However, that influence did not lead me to San Francisco or Coney Island, but to Ulvsunda Place. Homeward, if you like. From there the journey could start, three minutes from the subway, which in those days was a poetic mode of travel.

My earliest poems came into being amid the scents of naphthalene, sandalwood paste, gun grease, horse manure, hay, and sodden straw. They were written during my military service as a mounted light cavalryman with the K4 (Fourth Cavalry) battalion in Umeå. I had imagined a future as an artist, but the Swedish cavalry was ill-suited to oil painting. On the other hand, it was a splendid milieu for writing poems. The generously assigned stable duty offered good opportunities for contemplation. But it wasn't in K4's nightly stable watches that I wrote the suite of prose poems "From the Royal Norrland Dragoon Regiment," which was included in my first published collection. My early poems were soulful outpourings of a fairly common type, which revealed nothing of the stench of dung in their place of origin. The prose poems about the cavalry were written a few years later when, during a recall for training maneuvers, I renewed my contact with this nearly extinct type of military unit.

At first I greeted enthusiastically the "new simplicity" that dominated Swedish poetry of the 1960s. But after a while I grew more and more skeptical. Far too much of what I saw as special about poetry vanished from the poems—the images, the music, the magic itself. I felt closer to the English poets who were gaining notice then through the small presses in London's poetry underground than I did to my Swedish colleagues. Poets such as Anselm Hollo and Tom Raworth generously supplied me with books and with information on what was happening in the new English and American poetry—a channel of communication that is still open. My distance from the Swedish cultural discussion increased further when I spent a year at the poetry workshop in Iowa City in 1968–69, in the midst of the American student revolt.

I have never doubted that it's my own life I am writing about. That the poems are colored by my imagination, edited, and given form makes them even more like me. Many of them are based on old memories. Isn't there a risk, then, of memory glitches? Certainly—of conscious as well as unconscious ones. But a memory that has persisted through the decades has done so because it carries an important meaning. If this meaning changes, then the change is part of a process of development both in the memory and in me. The change in fact makes the memory even more my own. The past is part of the present and like the present is in continuous motion.

This line of reasoning may seem paradoxical, since this selection includes three long poetic suites that portray people from different eras—Guillaume Apollinaire, the mad king Ludwig of Bayern, Dante Gabriel Rossetti. My endless counterfeit biography of Apollinaire came out of relaxed play that I engaged in between more demanding tasks. Its tempo was quick and a little herky-jerky, as in a silent film, if one can imagine a silent film in full color. The first versions of this suite were written at the end of the 1960s, and Apollinaire emerged there as something of a hippie hero, though it's scarcely possible to sum him up in a simple "Make Love Not War" formula. He pursued both war and love without experiencing any great contradiction—and he was badly wounded in both contexts. But I thought that Apollinaire would have valued slogans like "Power to the Imagination," and on the back cover of the version that was published in 1972 I compared him to the Beatles. The counterfeit biography has about the same relation to Apollinaire's poetry as the Beatle's light-caramel-colored "Yellow Submarine" has to Rimbaud's more desperate drunken boat.

At the same time, Apollinaire was a poet diametrically opposed to that period's Swedish poetry, in which a circus atmosphere wasn't very highly prized. His mixture of sensualism, melancholy, utopianism, and intoxication with life didn't suit the times. Apollinaire had been closely linked to Picasso and other modernist artists in Paris in the first decades of the twentieth century and had tried to capture their techniques and their motifs in his poetry, which is full of mournful acrobats and harlequins. This became an important inspiration for me—that it was actually possible to "translate" lessons from painting into poetry. Apollinaire was a poet one didn't have to approach worshipfully. He was a living model for those of us who weren't striving to become really great and venerable skalds, seers, and thinkers. He sauntered around on the boulevards and saw mysteries in broad daylight.

The suite of poems about King Ludwig of Bayern was written in a darker mood. When personal problems become far too burdensome I prefer to push them outside myself. Though "prefer" is a misleading word, since it hasn't been a conscious intention. At the same time I was careful to make sure that the historical setting was accurate. Only people who were very close to me have managed to recognize situations and emotional states. The historical form made it possible for me to lie my way closer to the truth. Meanwhile, no one needed to feel singled out, not even I myself.

Apollinaire I had studied and translated before I began to manipulate his biography. About King Ludwig I had only vague and fragmentary knowledge. In 1976, at the Danish art museum Louisiana, I saw an exhibition of work by the German painter Klaus Liebig. One canvas gripped me. It portrayed King Ludwig drowning in Lake Starnberg (Starnberger See). But Liebig had doubled the king. Two identical kings held each other by the throat as they sank into the frigid water. I had no intention of writing a whole poetic suite on the subject, but I scribbled down some lines inspired by the painting.

> The one who's stopping his hands from swimming
> is he himself.
> The one who's weighing down his feet
> is he himself.
> Clamping his own throat
> he sinks
> into his own lake.

Later I began reading more about the mad king who had lived entirely in his dream worlds. He built his fantasy castle amidst the Alps; dressed as Lohengrin he glided out into his artificial grotto at Linderhof in a swan-shaped boat; and he used large portions of the public treasury to support Wagner and to build up Bayreuth in his honor. As I wrote I listened to Wagner's music, which I had always loathed, and I studied the Germanic and Celtic myths that underlay his operas. Much of what I had written about poetry had been in defense of the creative imagination, which had decidedly not seized power in the Swedish cultural debates of the 1970s. Usually it was described as a "flight from reality." Now, in a mixture of insight into myself and self-directed irony, I had identified myself with a person who had definitely fled reality until one night he drowned in his own lake. I think the poetic suite about Apollinaire embodies the light sides of my personality. King Ludwig represents the nocturnal.

At the beginning of the 1980s I felt I had gotten stuck in the genres of role poem and narrative ballad. The poem with the detailed title "Agatha Christie, Missing for Twelve Days in Sussex, Disguised as Her Husband's Lover"[15] marked the culmination of this form of costume poetry, but also my taking leave of it. The poem is based on an episode in Agatha Christie's life: when she found out that her husband was cheating on her, she arranged her own disappearance with all the cunning she exercised in her books. She hid out in a bed-and-breakfast in an English country town, where she registered under the name of her husband's lover—while the press and the police searched for her in vain. Naturally it wasn't a matter of disappearance but of an attempt to make a poem out of her own life. My decision was similar when I wrote the poem. To perform masquerading as a woman who in her turn was disguised as another woman—that was where I reached the limit. At that point I wanted to be myself again. That I had chosen as a persona a woman who in her writing had murdered an incalculable number of fictitious characters was no accident. I know. I betrayed my resolution to leave role poems behind a couple of decades later when I wrote *Salongsstycken* (Parlor Music) about Dante Gabriel Rossetti. But I am no fundamentalist.

We gladly identify with the greatness of the past. Even though we realize that much of the contemporary poetry that is now praised will soon end

15. "Sussex": Harding intended to write "Surrey," but in fact Surrey was where Christie's husband had gone to meet his lover. Christie went to Yorkshire, where she was located after ten days of mysterious absence.

up on the enormous literary garbage heap, we are reluctant to identify with the poets found in footnotes and the yellowed pages of scrapbooks. Only one episode in Dante Gabriel Rossetti's life—an utterly pathetic one—has been etched into common memory: how his wife Elizabeth Siddal takes her life with laudanum and how in despair he puts the manuscript containing the poems he's written to her into her coffin. Some years later, when he wants to include them in a book, he is forced to have her grave opened. Aside from this event, most of his life is as forgotten as his work. Few people show any interest now in the poems that once saw the light of day in such a dramatic fashion. Nor is Rossetti's painting any longer held in high esteem. His paintings of women with cascades of black or golden hair are probably better known as illustrations on greeting cards than as trailblazing works of art. His almost vampire-like fascination with long, white, exposed necks now seems at best merely typical of his era. After the death of his wife Rossetti led a more and more self-destructive life, for a time living with the bizarre poet Algernon Charles Swinburne in a house full of exotic animals. One of the main themes in *Salongsstycken* is that not only does passion decay, but also the poems that once expressed it meet the same fate.

The poetry I have written has most often been of the type that gets called "expanding," a term for a style that sets language in motion so that each line leads to the next through associations. I believe this comes of the conviction I have always had that poetry is a struggle against those mechanisms that limit us and prevent us from growing. But to tie a poem to a person or a narrative was also a form of limitation. In *Stjärndykaren* (The Star-diver), 1987, I developed a more exploratory style. I wandered further from the main theme and out into freer improvisations. Often I didn't even reveal this, just as I never identified the quotation from Nietzsche that lay behind the title poem. Nietzsche has never been among my favorite philosophers, but one line from *Thus Spake Zarathustra* became a sort of wandering lodestar for my new aesthetic: "I tell you: one must still have chaos in one, to give birth to a dancing star."[16] The name Zarathustra, as a matter of fact, can be taken to mean not the star-diver, but indeed the star-dancer. In the poem "Stjärnmålvakt" (Star-goalie) I had predicted that this figure would be resurrected in another universe "as the star-diver." This new, more unpredictable poetry in which associations were free to drift became that other universe.

16. *Thus Spake Zarathustra: A Book for All and None*, trans. Thomas Common (Edinburgh and London: T.N. Foulis, 1911), 12 (First Part: Zarathustra's Prologue: 5).

The associative style set its mark on my next two collections of poems as well. But little by little, more down-to-earth poems also began to force their way in. Every artist eventually reaches his own simplicity, claimed Paul Valéry. But he hastens to add that "all simplicity in art becomes fatal as soon as we regard it as a goal in itself and thus tend not to exert ourselves."[17] These words had a strong effect on me—surprisingly enough, since I had in my youth spent so much time writing polemics against the simplicity of Swedish poetry in the 1960s. Now I approached with open eyes precisely a "new simplicity," but one that I experienced as my own. After forty years I had written my way back to my starting point. I hope that the poems along the way have, not without considerable effort, gathered up some of what I have learned about the world, poetry, and myself.

17. "Autour de Corot," in *Pièces sur l'art* (Paris: Gallimard, 1934), 131. I have translated from the Swedish so as to convey the quotation as Harding encountered it. The French reads: "La volonté de simplicité dans l'art est mortelle toutes les fois qu'elle se prend pour suffisante, et qu'elle nous séduit à nous dispenser de quelque peine."

Guarding the Air

from *Flowers for James Dean*

1969

The Northwest Express

to my wife and to Blaise Cendrars

even in our sleep there are cables
between us. we are coupled
to each other like the railway cars
on their way to the sea

outside the window
Holland
a white van
on a winter's morning
filled with warm bread

startled from sleep I write this
instead of kissing you
you awaken in my poem
and give a bewildered smile

in a garbage dump they're burning books
and old streetcars. last night I discovered
a bird between your thighs. when the moon appeared
it flew out through the compartment window

the stars passed by at low altitude
they were made of glass or metal
and hummed like faulty fluorescent tubes.

December 1967

It Is Evening When You Turn Back

1.

the dead man is still hanging
from the crystal chandelier in the dining room. his black
patent-leather shoes graze your hair as you
eat dinner

the gendarmes have moved in. they write out
arrest warrants on the tablecloths, which they tear
into strips and roll into their typewriters
you see it all clearly, like one who returns
from a trip and sees his apartment again
after a long time

they've been waiting here for many years
playing cards on the floorboards
and squirting soda-water onto the bedbugs.

the police captain moves a chess piece
"stranger, as you pass by …"

2.

there's no such thing as time. everything's happening now
and inside you. that summer
you think was long ago is happening now
and inside you

you are five years old you are ten
you are twenty-eight and are still sitting there
leafing through a pile of old weeklies from 1916

when the aeroplanes were big butterflies
with red white and blue circles on their wings
and the American doughboys were little tin soldiers
with leggings and scout hats

you built a marionette theater
out of old cigar boxes

(the warm smell of old cigar boxes
and the bumblebees outside the window)

3.

the Indians stand ranged on the horizon
wrapped in their blankets. they are waiting

the little scout-soldiers have surrounded them
the small butterfly-planes buzz in the air

they drop fire from the sky
the Indians catch fire one after another

you look out the window
the horizon is smooth again

4.

there is no order other than the one
you create yourself. everything is one huge mess
and is happening now and you can't open
the window

the farmers outside are wearing blue overalls
and have strings in their hands. you pull
on the strings and they rise high
above the green earth. you're hanging
from a string in the marionette theater. a lonely child
is speaking above your head while the grass is dying
outside the window

engines shut off, the aeroplanes disappear behind the sun

5.

he passed his hand across the chess board
swept all the pieces onto the floor
"you don't understand this. you haven't
mastered the tactics of the game"

"cut down the body" he continued
in his monotone voice

The Train in the Background Is the Rock Island Line

St. Anselm Hollo crosses the Iowa River
on horseback. the grass is green
his head among the clouds.   singing
no   laughing bing bong bong   it was
the bells from the white city hall
with the gilded roof and the two flags
in Iowa City

when I shaved this morning I heard organ music
through the window,   foreign hymns
and the washbasin full of shaving lather and stubble
you had a cold but told me how you'd seen
your dead father in a dream and he explained
that he'd discovered *le jazz hot* and found it interesting

the water is blue. you must be brothers, said
the Indian temple-dancer. it was the blue
of our eyes.   that's why I talked about you
when I meant to talk about myself

all these buildings are stage flats
there is nowhere to go
                                    you go anyway
across a river that doesn't mean a thing

Captain Blood

for Che Guevara

it's Tuesday night on TV and they're
showing *Captain Blood.* the ship approaches
off the coast.   he stands on the bridge
and observes the fort through his telescope
it's impossible says the helmsman they have
over fifty cannon against our eight. they're holding
five of our men prisoner says Captain Blood

(we interrupt for a brief commercial message
the goddess of liberty pops up on the screen with her hair
full of curlers. it's some new
detergent. she rubs and rubs
the spots won't come out. it's some old
stage play)

a doctor   what this country needs is
a doctor. the ship comes closer   glides
slowly past sleeping marinas
north of Miami. he sits on the first-aid cabinet
in the prow and oils a pistol. his clothes
are full of dead insects. he coughs softly
and the wind fills the sails

hello gringos. "green grow
the hills" you sang when you marched
across the border with your pockets full of
greenbacks. the ocean is red. it's
the sunrise. someone has put a burning
cigar in the bottom corner of the star-spangled banner
it's morning. the stars grow pale
one by one

We All Saw Him

eastward, someone said. we
can't travel eastward and come to
San Francisco. the day after that
General Custer was elected president
and we fled the cocktail parties
and passed through fifteen states and it started raining
as it does in poems
when something important has happened

the car was full of people. namely
David and Daisy and Anselm and Hannes
and Arlene and Marybeth and Lotta and
Jan Szczepanski. our pockets were full
of potato chips and premixed drinks
in small medicine bottles but no one
was really grooving. we continued westward
in the dawn and the rain kept up and would
keep up for four years

we stuffed the newspaper where General Custer stood on his
white marble steps in his white marble city
crowning the year's Miss White Cherry Blossom
into our boots to keep out
the damp. it was too late. everywhere
we saw dead Indians like enormous bloody
birds among the cornfields

when we pitched camp on the river bank we saw him:
Crazy Horse. we were in the night
west of the Mississippi. flowers were growing
from his armpits. we saw his sperm   a white cloud
coursing through the Universe

The Blockade Is Broken, But to What End?

we went sledding backwards under
the starry sky. there was one star
for each state and many others that were
coming out. in a field a fanatical patriot
is painting red stripes on the snow
while others pile out of trucks and build
a palisade around a chewing-gum factory. we turned off
our flashlights and America disappeared

the dawn comes and reveals a turquoise-colored
house on the horizon. good morning Gordon
good morning Gisela. what sort of boat is that
coming up the river? we thought spring
was coming our way but it's the Monitor that sputters up
among the ice floes and fires in all directions
we make hot chocolate in the snow and hear the children
waking up around us

sleep! I shout but don't believe it'll work
besides, I can't be heard in the din from the cannon
and the first sunbeams. there is
another sound too, like the screeching of a violin
I wonder if it's the sound of my sled
or Charlie Chaplin crying into his
outsized shoes

On the Way to Little Big Horn

when we got closer we noticed that
the long line of cars wasn't moving.
all the cars were driverless wrecks
but their cracked headlights were still casting
their beams westward. in their back seats
kids were sobbing hysterically. the young
woman who'd lost her husband blew her nose
and said she'd gotten so ugly

I got scared when the dogs jumped up
onto me. the large white hairless albino
German shepherd had always made me wary
the policeman who turned up out of nowhere had
a cowboy hat on his head or was it
Lord Baden-Powell turning up in a snowstorm
with a flashlight in his hand?

there was nothing to be done. we wrote a letter
to the drugstore and ordered two bottles
of red wine and a box of bullets. "My husband
could have helped you," said the woman but it was
a lie. in any case he was dead or with
his girlfriend in St. Louis. I put my ear to the ground
and felt my head filling up with the rumble of
thousands of horses heading our way

Rebel without a Cause

I've come out of this film
once before. it was in Stockholm
a spring day on Birger Jarl Street over
ten years ago. it's fall in Iowa City
and this time the film doesn't end
when I come out onto the street. the police sirens
are still wailing and I am ten years older

I find George Kimball at The Mill
with his head on the bar. the fish
are drifting around obliviously in the fish tank
wedged between the display bottles. just when

he was about to throw himself from the car
he discovered that his sleeve was caught on the door handle
down below was the sea   in Technicolor blue

he puts some nickels in the jukebox
some more in the telephone. no one answers
but someone starts singing. George
this poem is never going to end
or it will end as idiotically as the film
(Mom Dad this is Jude)

I see his head right under the backlit beer ad
from the land of sky-blue waters. it's still
talking to me   what's the name of that song again
"I Know Where I'm Going"   that's truly fine

from *The Eagle Has Landed*

1970

20 July 1969—1944

I'm as naked as Apollo
                    in the bathtub. weightless
in the green water. the eagle
                    has landed. I
          think of Count Stauffenberg. 25 years today
                    since your failure
          your exploding briefcase in the eagle's nest
which merely revealed
                    that the man in the Wolf's Lair
     wore white long johns
                    in mid-summer. the eagle
                         has landed   so it's still alive
like the little man
          in the long johns
that historic day. it
     makes me too feel
                    somewhat important in the bathtub
                         where I'm writing this poem
                    to usher in the space age. I
     let go of the rim of the tub
                         in order to follow the news
          but can't forget you
                    Count Stauffenberg
               your failure   on this day
                    when the eagle succeeded
                         and put its footprint
                              on the Sea of Tranquillity

Vietnam

there's always just a thin wall
separating us from them. they are
closer to us
than the leaves and the rain here. you start over
from the beginning:
"we're all in it
together. our hair
flows together …"
THE RAZOR BLADE
"our arms grow outward
from the same body …" through everything that's said
you can hear the rattle of a typewriter
or a machine gun
it grows louder. it
disturbs me as I go around
painting haloes on all the people
lining up at the bus stop.
makes the calm more real
like death here. like
the leaves here. they're burning
even before they've fallen from the trees
only now does the helicopter
become visible up there
against the blue. a body
that's thrown out
that falls
twists in the air. a face
that sees
the sky. the earth
only not you
a face. it could not
just as easily
be yours

Rockets

these rockets
            exploding in the sky tonight
announce that the 70s have begun. it's the stars
        that are exploding. in the cities of the 60s
                no one's home anymore. everywhere
the sound of explosions
        and people screaming. you find yourself
                in a world
                    where only the cars evolve
            become shinier and more beautiful. grow
                    into gigantic chrome-clad metallic monsters
            that attack one another
                    crush one another. you too
if you don't change. you walk along the highway
        with a shopping bag
                in each hand. far away
            ditches cross
        where the bikers lie buried
    where are the people
            who were supposed to invent the words
                more important than silence? only then
can the screams fall silent
            here all roads lead to the sea
        where once again the rockets are burning starfish
        that send the false signal:
                "everything's o.k."

Puberty

was it at the Palace of Sport in 1952? a whole school class
disappeared into the green water
they don't surface again
until today
and I feel the strong smell
of chlorine in my nostrils. we were locked up
like all the dusty birds
in the biology room. all exits barred
by a white-clad lunchroom matron
who filled the whole world
with her enormous bosom
by teachers and
officers in the reserves. law
and order. there was nothing else to do
but let the air out of Mr. Fürstenberg's bike tires
and wander off and get lost
whenever we had orienteering
year after year
the boy in the Tarzan swimsuit
has been bouncing up and down on the trampoline.
howling in a shrill breaking voice
he dives into the water
to gaze in silence
at the girls' legs. but they're already married
and all rolled up in lilac bathrobes

Für Janet Persson

heute ist es strahlende Sonne
      und wolkenloser Himmel. German grammar
          is eternally unchangeable
            like old classmates. we all
        had a classmate once
    who was named Janet Persson
         and who wrote letters
            to *Bildjournalen*
asking
    how to become a stewardess. der Himmel
ist so blau
      so blau. we knew
        you would never
           manage it. so
          many who never manage it. your
          hands were too big
    through the climbing frame
    in the gym you're still
           looking toward the sky. high up there
       floats
         die Lufthansa. down here
   you are slowly burning
       yourself up
in a hopeless protest
       against loneliness

Janet Persson noch einmal

in your childhood
the rain flows down the tile roofs
     of Ulvsunda Street
       and a stream of children in blue gym suits
      flows over a leather-covered "horse"
while a whistle screeches irritably. Blue
     gym shoes across the varnished floor. they
       pass by in silhouette
        as at a shooting range

play hopscotch on one foot
     between *life* and *death*. a gaudy marble
       rolls straight across the sidewalk
       knocks over a tin soldier

1954 and the jackdaws scream above the ridgepoles
    the guys in the neighborhood feel up her breasts
      over and over behind the auto repair shop "Goddammit!
       Goddammit!" she hisses
    but comes back every day. they
can't figure out if she likes it or not
and she knows
    that they will never dare to kiss her
  never. never
it's Tuesday 5 o'clock
      and there's a smell of fried Falun sausage
     from an open lighted window. in the background
  the scornful grating laughter
from an old Dodge

she gives back to her childhood
    a frayed jump-rope, a blue gym suit
        a couple of bookmarks with pink angels
            and the Motala radio station. she
      keeps going, through banks factories parking garages
a gigantic marble
    comes rolling toward me

Umbrella

then there was the guy who married
an umbrella. at night
        she hung on a hook
    upside down like a dead bat
in the silent hallway. what
            did she dream? what does
        a newly married umbrella dream about?

rain. like a black sun
    she glistens in the dark rain
        twirls in hubcaps
            is reflected in windshields
        and he can walk through the rain
    in dry clothes

        Stockholm's central station stands there
    full of light inside—a monument
to someone who left
                one rainy Thursday

it was the day after the divorce. his clothes
    were soaking wet

I Decide to Take Up the Battle against
Bonnier's Literary Magazine

even the yellow bus
was delayed by the snow and slush
fantastic! today
everything's late
all synchronization has stopped. the adventure
begins right here. poetry
wasn't born in Uppsala. it
exists wherever
someone runs across the street
against a red light
all buses
roll toward the unknown. in my pocket
I have a ticket for tomorrow
and I'm not afraid
the whole city
a chaos of honking cars. trumpet fanfares!
I hop off at St. Eriksplan
and my mustache is burning
like a Bengal light
in the sleet

from *Search Line*

1972

The Confused Teacher of the Deaf

The sound of rain on the metal windowsill
where the sparrows' small black claws land
scratch away
a little of the green paint
will always carry it with them
I too carry
some green color under my feet.

A gull blows in under the bridge
moving backwards, like a wet paper bag.
I end up there too, want to have
all that concrete
above my head. Here everything is shadow,
the foliage dark green, the wheels of the subway cars
squeal above my head. In this din
no one can hear me if I speak
and I do speak.

Wet and green, like the trees
surrounding the silent playground games at the school for the deaf.
He stood at the window
and crumbled a piece of chalk. Their eyes
followed his lips, their eyes
locked onto the blue sparks
around the clapper of the bell
while the room filled
with unheard clanging signals.

(When he turns away and speaks
they can't see his lips, don't understand
a thing. and he does turn away.)

Write as I dictate
   he says:

We must think new thoughts together
   new thoughts
      we can only think together.
Our heads
   move forward through the world, words
      pass through our mouths
make everything visible
      keep us warm.

         The din from subway car after subway car
      passing through my head.
   The bells clang. LEAN OUT
THE WINDOW! You move forward, move
   homeward. Only those who stand still
      move backward
               outside the window.

      They look at him. Is he speaking
   the wrong language? Making the wrong signs?
He suddenly looks totally confused
   as if he were filling up with darkness from the inside
         and he writes with chalk
on the bridge's concrete arch
   on the blackboard: *The earth is standing still*
         it's me that's spinning.

Search Line

1.

      Here at the edge of the forest each second becomes
   unimaginably large, each grain of sand
a boulder. Behind my back: potato fields
           small pink fists clenched in the clay
     waiting for birth, already living
  like the stones, slowly, in the dark
gradually changing.

In ikons children are born
  with faces radiating light.
Like staring at the sun
        and it will remain there
    even though the darkness is creeping in
  from the edges. At night I hear
our children wake up and cry. I saw them being born
  in blood, being washed
    and laid on clean sheets.
  The world grows into them
first Mama. They drink her in. No person
    is more important than you. Only the sun
  is more important than you.

2.

   To enter a tree
   pass through a tree.
   On the other side
   you are another person.

One can find one's way if one remembers
    that all trees are different. Flickering light
      from flashlights, dogs barking
    raised voices. The search line is combing the woods
for lost children.

      In red rubber boots they are making their way
    toward the east
      or the west, toward the north
or south, always deeper into the woods.
    The water rises in their boots
      makes their socks as wet
        as the moss in their pockets.

They will never return here.

3.

      I lie awake
    and hear them crying, hear how the woods
are growing into them. They drink water
      from black tarns, fall asleep
     among the bracken, wake again
at the shriek of the chain saws. Blue blades
    cut through their lives.

In the middle of the woods: the sound from a city. Car headlights
    peek out from the badger-burrows, children
      lonely and grieving
    as in large airports. It's the hour
when the dogs return
          panting
      with bloody strips of cloth in their jaws.

Great titmice call from the trees:

      Francis!

Children fall out of the trees.

      Francis!

Grandpa and the Little Old Ladies in Leksand

1.

    My mother's father was the best organist in the world.
He served
        school and church
    loyally for a thousand years. Finally died in 1927
hymn 424, verses 1–9. I thought of him
    today
        when I was rowing a skiff on Opplimen Lake.

        Our daughter is sick
    and is walking around with large wads of cotton
    in her ears. She drinks red medicine.
Grandpa drank fermented red currant juice
    behind the gooseberry hedge
        reading the organ hymnal.

The light is almost too strong here. We
    gaze at summer through the mosquito net
        a mourning veil
    full of broken-off fly-wings. On the pier
a perch
    is drying. It got the hook through one eye.
The others I throw back into the lake
    and they vanish downwards
        toward darker water
            leaving red trails of blood behind them.

Every thousand years
    a bird flies past me
        and reminds me
that one second of eternity

has been lost. Voices
reach me from the other shore
or from the clouds.

This blessèd day …

cumulus   cumulus

2.

Sacrifice to the forefathers. The water
carries me. The smell of cow
                hangs in the air. The water
        drips from their muzzles. The earth
is a body that's breathing
        like the cows' taut brown bellies
                filled with wet grass. For a thousand years
        their mournful eyes
have looked out across the lake.

                A workman in high rubber boots
            is cutting the rotted reeds
    with a scythe. "Dammit! Dammit!" he shouts.
Soon the whole lake will be overgrown. Gadflies
            bore into the cows' hides
        lay their eggs
in the summer's meat
            which quickly darkens.

1921. Grandpa opened all the doors
    of the organist's house
            to let the animals
        come in and drink.

3.

All the little old ladies in Leksand
     loved him far into the 60s
filled the whole church
          with their sighs. Heavy breaths
     that drowned out my own
as if the church itself
               were gasping for breath. The rims
of their eyes were blood-red
     as if from a fish-hook. At any rate
          there were too many of them.
Some of them had to give up.

          Slowly they moved
     through the summer
     dressed for a different century, sat
in the garden at Korstäppan
          and talked about him
               while their world filled up
     with tourists. Everywhere
men in shorts with bare chests
who smelled of sweat in the dairy shop, good God
                    even in church.

The workman is still tramping around in the reeds
          and shouting: "It's rotting! it's
               getting rottener every day!"
On the road a truck passes by
     carrying milk bottles. I understand
          their clinking against each other.

          Now the noise from J. O. Wallin falls silent. Now
     the little old ladies are falling silent one after another
collapsing
          in their back yards, changing

into little hillocks. Their pots full of potatoes
        go on boiling
    inside on their stoves, day after day
black soot.

4.

"Meddysin's yucky!" The mountains
    breathe slowly around us
        also the pines
            and the walls of the buildings. His suit
        grows greener every year
    in the chest with the mothballs. Also
resting there are some dead wasps
            from which year?

        They are dead now
those little old ladies. It is impossible
    to live in a song. Their braids
        are young again, their bodies
    as light as the wasps, vanishing downwards
toward darker water. "Yucky!"

Martin Luther
    why didn't you ever visit the old-age home
        disguised as a young organist?

Now she's sleeping
    our daughter. My wife
        is nursing our other daughter. Everyone
    has to join in, live on
in a song.

I open the doors
    to our house.

September

Sunny September afternoon, yellow leaves
on Kindstu Street. Huge steel clamps
in every second house. Otherwise they'd burst
from all the life inside them.
A frayed poster
USA OUT OF INDOCHINA in red and blue. Many
have died so that you might be born, this
unites you with those
who are dying right now.

Everything's burning. It burns
with white flames. The cobblestones are cold
have a thin layer of moisture
like eyes
but they don't see you. The houses see you.
You can go in and out of them.

Death lives in the empty spaces
between the houses, in the empty spaces
between people. There are large empty spaces
between us. When we die
we enter them.

Here there is still wind. I
take it into my lungs. The bells are ringing.
The wind makes them swing
back and forth
and then not back.
Watch out!

Europe—A Winter Journey

1.

We came here
as one comes to a library
to find warmth. All we found
was silence, books   and silence.
We're at the start of a thousand-year Reich.

Hotel Europe: the curtains are faded summer dresses
from the 30s. You wake up
in the middle of the night. They've stolen your dreams
replaced them with lies. On the radio
someone shouts in a slick voice
that here in Dachau
we have so much snow
that it's just crazy!

It smells like a bicycle repair shop
where someone is kneeling in a trench coat
patching a flat tire. Enormous piles
of valve stems
in the sunshine 25 years ago.

We could put on our helmets
but they wouldn't protect us
just make our heads
heavier.

2.

Where do the explosions come from? He thought
they came from inside him. There was no reason
                    to interrupt the preparations
            for the pop-music festival
        but people removed the flower pots
from their windows.

He went back to bed, rolled up inside the map of Europe
            while his dreams passed by
        like trains full of soldiers on leave
    somewhere between death and Hollywood.

You see the parking lot here.
That's where his house was.

3.

            Your feet are cold as you look at
        the naked woman on the poster kiosk
Dann nehmen wir ein Saunabad!
            Long rows of naked women
        in the snow. Barracks. You stamp
your feet to keep warm
            and the echo multiplies between the buildings
                grows louder
        and comes back at you
            millions of feet
                come back.

Miss Universe. They've stolen her too. Her smile
        glitters in the dark between two camera flashes. Winter streets
            full of spangles. Stars fall

go out
        light up again
    when she moves before us
    at a speed of three smiles a minute.
Inside the newsreel camera
        it all coils up
    into a long snake of celluloid.

Auf wiedersehen my dear, they sang. Their heads
    seemed so small
        in the huge collars of their uniforms.

4.

Berlin. Munich. Prague. I look into Europe
    as into the guts of an old radio:
        dusty vacuum tubes and copper wires, cathedrals
            and rusty barbed wire. Dust. Dust
        the smell of musty old radio programs.
    Und jetzt
        meine Damen und Herren
playing
        especially for you tonight
            The Ghetto Swingers
        from Theresienstadt!

They play "On the Sunny Side of the Street." The sunbeams
    descended between the bookshelves. I
        was only five then
    and thought the potted plants
would grow until they filled the whole room
        like the voice on the radio
        that spoke about unconditional surrender.
A car has stopped on the Autobahn. They open the hood

and the insides spill out
as from an animal being gutted.

Somewhere between Hanover and Paradise
something very important has been lost.
Therefore they have to keep playing. When they stop playing
everything will be frozen. They
must keep playing....

5.

Hear how our voices echo. We
are inside the *Tirpitz* now. The black oil
fills me. Thousands of corpses
go gliding around in full uniform.
Deep inside the rusty hull
there's a wallet with a photo of a girl.
I'm talking about the moment before the torpedo.
That's where we move in.
Her lips are shaped into a scream.

6.

You wake up in a hotel room
in the middle of Europe. 150,000 children
are waiting to be born tonight. We
ought to sit up in bed
and talk about them, sit here
and talk to each other
as seriously as children.

What can a person say? I said: Hang on.
        Time has been transformed into a room
     where we move in, hang up
   our clothes. The lamp here will shine
as long as the stars.

We're at the start of a thousand-year Reich.

The panic-stricken commander of Westerplatte
   continues to fight his own war.

from *Ballads*

1975

Cape Farewell

1.

Where tattered clouds flutter
like the Union Jack on the icebound steel ship,
where the captain looks through the telescope
at black salt water, records essentials:
"The 11th of July the ice was in strong motion."
68° north latitude
where Europe goes under imperceptibly, where
King Christian ix Land
is steadily reconquered by silence.

Reach solid ground 20 July 1888 (Fridtjof Nansen)
on the east coast of Greenland. To travel
across a totally white sheet of paper
where the words become a long trail
that will be crossed by others, will keep going
in many directions. To recover
everything that existed
before we gave it a name
before our words
were united with the continents. And the continents
will live in our words
if we recover them.

In February 1973
I'm sending out a poem
to bring back the white silence.

2.

The seals saw them coming. The gulls
    saw them coming, from the east
        through the drift ice. Humans
    in sealskin clothing saw them, perhaps. In 998.
Thorgils Orrabeinsfostri is shipwrecked
            in the drift ice, comes in toward the coast
    with his wife
and his men, lives four winters
and four summers "undir Grænlandsjöklum
            í vík nokkurri við sandmöl."

    To find a mountain
    and give it a name, find a rift in the ice
and give it a name, find words that become real
        as food, pass through the silence
    to recover on the other side
what can fill it, pass through the cold
            to recover the warmth.

Thorgils. The knife flashes in his hand. Flensed seals
    fall out of their skins, words
        as weighty as the speaker
            red and meaty
newborn babies. Thorgils cuts his nipple
    nurses his newborn son
            with blood.

The sun too is a word
    glowing above the snow.

3.

In the cold
there is only one thought: the cold.
Shoes think it in ski bindings
      one centimeter off the ground. Dry bone-heaps
        and collapsed huts think it
    under the snow. Many are those
           who have filled their lives with snow.

Behind you the shiny round Eskimo women, naked
    in the huts, the shape of seals. Behind you
      the sled-dogs' panting
           and their long blue tongues. Behind you
      a dry crack of gunpowder
      in cold air
    and a bird falling
heavily to the ground. You return
with strange stones and sketched maps, notebooks
      full of snowmelt and numbers.

To stand in the cold
    with red knuckles cracked
      inside your mittens. To stand in the window
        and scream silence
    into yourself.

On the other side of the white fields
    you will find new words, new bodies
      find the words that will make the northern lights
    into a mighty tree of light

growing through the universe, wave after wave
 of light growing
  sprouting new buds, perpetually new branches.

In each word
 you will be reborn.

An Evening at Home with William Blake

1.

Even as a child he drew people
    the way they looked, like houses
        with long legs
    that began under their chins. They
grew upward out of the ground
    the way grandfather clocks grow from the floor
        and tables and chairs from the parquet. Houses
            are built from the inside, built
        from the bottom up, by hands
    that stretch upward from the earth. They grow upward
from dark cellars.

And this house around you
    is hell, and this house around you
        is the law, is power over you. Inside it
        people buy and sell you.

        The lines in his forehead know
        that the Tyger's time must come
    before the Lamb's, that there are other words than those
that fill the mines with children
        and the colonies with soldiers
        in red coats. The engraving wheel
    cuts lines in the metal. The world's contours
are etched forever in the acid bath, his veins
            in the grain of the wallboards.

    Walls around us. Walls
inside us. Shut in
    we talk to a wall

talk to a wall
    inside us.

2.

    William Blake's wife lifts the iron
from the stove, carries it to the table. Heavily
        it slides over the damp shirt
            over warm wet cloth. His thoughts
          are so heavy. They've gotten stuck in the clothes
     which are so full of thoughts
that they will never be really clean again.

She comes over to him
    lies down next to him on the bed.
        Their shoes meet under the bed
in front of the porcelain chamber pot
     with the border of green flowers. His member
        pushes in between her thighs
among the soft curly hairs, pushes into
    the moist cleft
       where the Universe is created, slippery wet walls
     tauten and relax. The Universe pulsates
with their movements
         from star to star
          from darkness to darkness.

      Freedom streams in
     through their nostrils, opens
    doors and window shutters, draws the wind
   through the chimney
so the fire flares up. A wind goes

through the houses, shakes them
　　　so the pots and pans fall down
　　　　　from their racks.

　　　Only their heavy breaths
　　　distinguish them from the darkness
　　until it too begins to breathe sharply
dies and is born again, is filled by light
　　　that grows up around them. Another house
　　　　　where the sky flows blue through the windows
　　where clouds glide through the rooms, the floor
turns green and is covered by flowers
　　　　　　when his seed falls on it.

Shudders and the creaking
　　　from the bed, soft fluids
　　　　　run between their thighs. For one second
　　it was they who made the Universe grow
made people rise up and move onward, tree roots
　　　　　push deeper down into the earth
　　　seeking water.

3.

　　　The same grizzled God
his muscular body covered by silvery down.
　　　　　The same white Goddess
impregnated by a stream of stars.
　　　　　The same rain
in the plow-furrows. The ox-driver's call
　　　　　forces the plow through the earth
　　　with the power of brown muscles.

The same sun
fettered among the tree-branches.
        The same face
nailed to a tree trunk. The same blood
        on the wet clay
so that everything might move onward
            so that the new Albion
        might rise
from the Sea of Time.

4.

    With the window shutters thrown open
their house fills with light. Their brains burn
            like lamp chimneys overheating, burn up
        the air in the room, light up
the whole city. Enormous felines
                    emerge from the alleys
                show street urchins
                    the way home.

This is the start of the Age of the Tyger. The cries
        of the crowds stream in through the windows.

            When the walls give way inside you
            the walls of the Bastille will fall. When
        the walls give way inside us
we will become a single vital power
            that rifle bullets cannot harm
        not a river but an ocean
like time, not a river
                but an ocean.

Tomorrow or in a thousand years
we will open the roof hatch
   and stand up
  our faces to the sun, rise up
 from our houses
as from rotted caskets. Tomorrow
or in a thousand years
   we will get to live the lives
  we were intended to live. William Blake
blows out the light. Tomorrow
  we will color the pictures,
    he says.

Lasse-Maja at Carlsten Fortress

1.

Every night the water rises again, every night
he is flooded by his own blood
        which fills him with darkness, every night
        the beard stubble pushes out harshly
from his virginal cheeks. Where to escape to
        when all paths lead into oneself, lead
deeper into the mountain, gray walls
                that have grown from the boulders, gray stone
        arisen from the sea, granite walls
        granite clouds, waves of gray stone.

Every night the whole curséd island sinks
into the sea like a rat-trap, every night
        the prisoners crowd so close together in the stench
        that no one can tell
whose screams are keeping him awake. The chains
        bind them together, the chains
            and the sea and Bohuslän's cliffs
            from which they hack
                every day
                    new stone for their prison.

2.

Hell, once
        he too was transformed, like the sea,
            from man into woman, once
            he sailed out smoothly

in blue skirt and white lace. One day
he stole the whole world
stuffed it in his mouth
and swallowed it. He
ate up the whole world
until a glow the green of bottle-glass
appeared behind his eyes.

Ran like a madman
with the skirts in his hand,
through the woods along Lake Hjalmar, through
blackthorn bushes chattering with sparrows,
ran on white legs through the streams, down
into the beds of the girls and the boys too, expelled
his sperm with the church plate under the mattress, fled again
through back doors, chimneys, privy seats.
For everything existed in him: the blackthorn bushes,
the streams, man, woman, fire, filth.

Was finally stopped
by a wall, by a wall of stone
where no transformations are possible
except the last one, into stone. Gradually
life turns to fossil
to xylography, so gradually
that one doesn't know
if the people one is talking to
are alive or dead.

On the ramparts the blue-uniformed recruits
pace back and forth. Lasse-Maja spits
a long brown stream. Once
even the priest would kiss
this mouth of his. Lasse-Maja

dictates his *Memoirs* to the gulls
　　　　which squeal
　　　　　rudely but appreciatively.

3.

　　　　He found a tree
　　with a crown like an enormous green dress
that he climbed into. The dogs found him.
　　　　The sheriff and the ruddy-faced farmers
　　　　　gathered around the trunk. Slowly
　　　　　　he began the long climb
　　　　　　down to the ground.

Groaning in chains in the bottom of a black prison wagon
　　　that glides away
　　　　along a dark avenue
　　　while the crowns of trees float
across his face.

　　　　Goddamned
　　chains, the chains too
existed in him, and the stones. Every night
　　　　　they pull him down into the dark
　　　and every day
　　and every night: iron, stone. He
sinks slowly into himself, iron, stone,
　　while little by little the world
　　　　steals back everything else.

90

Grandma Grandpa and the Memory of Jenny Wilkas

The younger I get the easier it is
to stand erect, even when the ceiling
droops above me. It's harder
the older I get
to enter these old rooms
from which I was gradually born.
But every detail of them
remains in me. A click
and the roll of film slowly turns
inside my head.

Pictures of the house on the road to Uddevalla. The two gables
facing the main road, painted white. On the other houses
rough gray planks. Grandma
with blue gown and hairnet. The cabinet
with racing trophies, a silver-gray suit of armor against oblivion
in a murkiness as muted as the clatter
from the horses' hooves, as the memory of ripped-up parimutuel slips
on the gravel. Grandpa was long since dead
no longer stood blustering on his stable-grounds.

In the attic, stock certificates, Kreuger & Toll,
dusty moose antlers, boots, hunting guns, even shells,
Gyttorps brand. For a thirtieth of a second the house is filled
by the darkness from inside the camera.

Cerebral hemorrhage—Grandma raised the coffee cup
but didn't put it back down. Her eyes
started looking inward. With a faraway voice
she said: "Why are there
so many black stars?"

I was ten years old, stared at her.
      The big pieces of furniture rushed at me
         but fell down helplessly on the floor
   with all four legs sticking up. The lupines
grew in over everything, long black slugs
                  on the well-lid.

Then she put the cup down again: "I was
      so far away." Was her brain filled with smoke
         blossoming puffing silent smoke? Did she
            spin around in there
                  in a huge centrifuge
               until sharp beams
         straight from inside her
   suddenly cast her back up
like a diver from the water? So far away
            and now back
         in a light as translucent
   as an electric bulb lit in the middle of the day.

            And what remained
         from before the fall of Kreuger & Toll? The memory
   of the horses. Jenny Wilkas in a fast trot
across frozen Brunnsvik Bay, Grandpa
            ruddy-faced in the sulky, the reins
         between his hands and the horse's head pulling
      forward in the snow-filled wind. The ice-flakes spraying
around the horseshoes, melting
         on the warm bodies of the horses.
On the other side of the main road
      the train went by. I counted the cars
         18 of them, dug blue clay from the ditch
      made model soldiers
            from the war I'd found
         in old weekly magazines from 1917.

They had sunk so deep in the clay
  that their shapes remained there.

The horses: that was something I knew about
   "covering the ground
on all fours again"
   above the clay
    so it wouldn't swallow me
     feet in the air
    and nonetheless on all fours
   like before,
back when I could still remember
the black stars
   but could not speak.

Danny's Dream

An aluminum angel
above the green weather maps.
With outspread wings
along a low-pressure ridge north of the Azores,
with glittering reflections in her goggles
the sun's propellers
in her blond hair
the flying ace Lita Lona rises
toward blue layers of air
where all clouds have been dispersed
by a distant saxophone.

Is she in your dream
or are you in hers? Was she born in you
or were you born to her?
When he puts the saxophone to his lips
he sees her coming in
toward the orchestra at low altitude, Lita Lona,
the Cold War's angel. His dreams
have always come back from outside, armed
like the model planes he built
out of balsa wood and Japan paper.
With clattering rubber-band engines
they turned and headed straight at him
or ended up hanging tattered in the apple tree
as fragile
as the world's cities.

The first time he saw her
was on a pinball machine. Silver wings
carried her and her two-engine amphibian
over the flashing, clicking mirror

where a metal ball roamed
like a police car crisscrossing New York
at night. In a briefcase in the cockpit
she has the plans for future nuclear wars,
Lita Lona,
as beautiful and unreal
as an X-ray of a skyscraper
around which swarm the skeletons of birds.

In the cities of the 50s her skirt billows up
above the hot-air grating
and the Communist threat stands in the green parks
wearing a trench coat
and passes military secrets inside cigarettes.
She lives in the great void
between yes and no
where silent conversations about absence
are exchanged by empty suits
in phone booths made of glass. In the shop windows
the mannequins' eyes are dreaming. Naked
they touch each other with unfeeling fingers
and signal with immovable arms
to taxis that do not stop.

Does she have eternal life
like one who stands at the top of a skyscraper
and balks at jumping? Faces shiny as quarters
turn upward. Before they know it
they're all on their way through the air
in flapping clothes
while their dreams leave them
in order to destroy the world. Lita Lona
puts on her flyer's helmet
and BZZZZZ she's under way
across the shiny surface of the water

foam churning around the pontoons.
  She smiles.
She whistles an old hit song, "Nagasaki."
She's oblivious to the enormous spider web
      where they will find her airplane
    the way one comes on a scrunched-up fork
  at a roadside diner.

When he takes the saxophone from his lips
  he is back in the dark
    where the stars are strewn across the sky
  like dandruff on the shoulders of tuxedos
at a multinational cocktail party.
    His head is empty, as deserted
    as summer-cottage country on a fall evening
  when the only bright glint is from a forgotten badminton net,
or a sports arena at night
      with long lines of chalk
        between which no one is running.

The Owl

At nine o'clock in the evening
two round eyes suddenly light up
      in the oak. A soft snapping sound
    and the tree is transformed into an owl
with feathers of rough bark, and talons
      of soil-encrusted root. Breaks free of the earth,
        a flying tree trunk, with heavy wing-beats
          low above the ground.

    Eyes that see
        how the darkness lives, the stones shine
and the june bugs glow on the trees, vast illuminated cities
      in the blueberry patch as golden maidenhair burns like phosphorus.
      A powerful cold stream of oxygen
    rushes through the woodland flowers. They burn together
until they're blown up from within by a terrific black heat
    explode
        into incandescent colors.

    It carries inside itself
the world as it was
    before the stars began to drift across the sky. It
      is heavy with earth. The thoughts of the dead
are alive in it. Little by little
          it sees the world being transformed
        into the world
      it carries inside itself.

The Black Death

1.

      Green at the outset, green
   and blue. A ship laden with English broadcloth
is swept against the cliffs outside Bergen. Under the surface
     a light-colored body glides
        through the dark water, breaks the surface
     establishes a link
  between the light and the depths. Laid out on the deck
bodies darken in the sun.

     Hang a piece of meat
     in a tree.
     When it turns black
     the plague is here.

And the ship with masts that have already begun to sprout leaves
  sails on
     through forests and mountains
       through days and nights, through
         cities and hamlets, breathing
      so labored that people pray to God
     that it will stop, rooms
  so cold that only the dead can endure them. Slowly
the roads disappear astern. Slowly
        the forests close up again.

    The tolling bells fall silent
and the ringing axes among the tree trunks. In the towers
     birds perch
       close, dense, black as the blood
     under people's nails. As silent
  as the darkness after a scream.

2.

Other days with cold white light, frozen days
    when you can walk on the water. Burbot
        frozen into the ice, their bearded faces
look at us with upturned eyes. We walk on the ice
        club their foreheads, chop them out
    with heavy crowbars. They
   are our forefathers. We eat them. Slowly
they begin to eat us from the inside.

        Deeper into the darkness
     until you become part of it
     until it becomes part of you. Down there
are other faces, more grotesque
                harder to make out.
           Yet unless you have looked into them
      you can never see the light.
In the nighttime they glide into your dreams
    eat your name
      until you are only a body
through which the dreams are coursing. Thick lips
      gaping round mouths and eyes
        swim through you, devour
          everything you want to be
      until you are yourself.

Now they start unloading the ship
    lifting large bales of cloth
from the darkness. All the signs are clear.
    A buzzard
hangs unmoving in the air
        is burnt into the sky.

3.

The first thing you see
is a little boy with a rake. He
is dressed in blue broadcloth. After him
comes a little girl
in tattered clothes. Gray light
washes over you.

They dig a ditch. They
throw the two children in
and quickly fill it up again. This
won't save anyone.
You open the door
and the darkness washes over you.

4.

And the harvest laborers with their sickles in hand—
the fields close around them, the trees
close around them. In the wet loam
their feet begin to shine and give their light
to the grain. Horses ramble unhindered
with bloody hoof-locks
and thistles tangled in their manes, cows
with heavy udders and bells around their necks
steadily further away.

In the Middle Ages everyone is dead
but they travel on inside the trees. The summer sky
is their sail, the bluest sail
in the world. Wind blows
through the crowns of the oaks. The air
from their lungs puts the foliage in motion.

And the voyage continues
        through seas of green leaves
      through waves
of dark earth.

Inside the acorns they sit huddled together.
      In small birchbark jugs they have lingonberry wine
           sweetened with honey. They take a swig now and then
      as history rolls on,
while they watch the quick-padding badger
         being slowly transformed into a pile of ashes.

5.

        And the woman by the sea
      misses her sailors. She
   was a cloud above the sea, existed there
long before their time
      like all the unborn
        who are crying out for bodies
     to be born in.

She is searching for her lovers, her nipples
      stare down into the deep. The whole sea
        flows into her
           in strong currents of blue-black water:
         jellyfish with burning hair
    the plaice's dotted suns, floating butterflies
blue-edged mackerel with silk-white bellies.

        Lusterless round opal-eyes
      loosen from the mute faces.
    White-gloved hands wave
swim off two by two. All that can be heard

is the starfishes' hearts tapping lonesome
in the nocturnal water.

She slits silver abdomens with her fingers, pink innards,
lets death into everything. Where are her lovers?
Her songs seek them out
in all the seashells on the shore.
In the songs they are still resting
heavily between her thighs.

6.

The Black Death arrives in winter
in a worn dog's-fur coat, with snowflakes in its eyebrows. Snow
swirls in its nostrils. Arrives bringing ice
to people's eyes, snow
to the cauldron on the hearth.

Arrives in summer
sneaking back from another direction,
sets a heather moor on fire. They cough in the smoke.
It comes back
in brown teeth and the smell of gruel
forces its knee between their thighs
and ties them up, knocks them to the ground
rushes into them
a vortex of snow
whirling into their warm bodies.

And the light streams through their houses
in summer. The darkness
in winter.

They flung
    burning logs at it. The howling
        from inside the flames, from the god
that lives in the fire. The silence
    from the white god
        that is the snow, which covers
    the cottages   the fields
covers the fever   covers the mountains
                heavy with stone.

7.

      And the ship sails through you. Dead hands
    hold the rudder. On warm days
filled with sun and wild honey
    you see the masts among the evergreens. The salmon
        fly up the mountains
           in great leaps, shining bodies
        through the spruce forests. You can
    not follow them. People are burning dead bodies
on the river bank. The smoke swirls away,
           a swarm of wild bees
              from a hollow tree trunk.

If you remove everything
    do you end up with light or darkness? You
        don't know. You want to keep everything.
In the darkness you see
    growing light. Inside the light
        yet another darkness. It is you
    staring out from the buzzard's eyes
and from the snake's. It twists
        between the sharp talons.
    In its eyes there flashes

your own cold gaze. The pattern of the tree branches
is identical to the pattern
in your palms.

The round church-walls
are an eggshell around the black crow
that eats them from the inside
stabs its beak through them
rises from them
with its wings smeared with egg-white and mortar.
Inside, the people of the future are already buried. The trees
are already growing straight through them.
Between the trunks a ship
with a dead crew is sailing.
They live in you, rise toward the surface in you.
You sink down into their darkness.

Jazz Poems

from various volumes

Buddy Bolden's Original Jass & Ragtime Band

1.

oh all the people just about went crazy when
Buddy Bolden's band played in Lincoln Park
in New Orleans the summer of 1893. yes all the whores
in New Orleans went nuts when Buddy played
If You Don't Like My Potatoes Why Do You Dig
So Deep and the young clarinetist from
The French Opera Alphonse Picou got so confused
that he started playing the piccolo part
in High Society on the clarinet and kept on
playing it without a break for forty-eight hours

Buddy Bolden sat in his barber shop
on Franklin Street and laughed his
head off. He understood that he
had found something completely new and he
called it *Jatz* or *Jass*. yes that's how
it began and it's still going strong

2.

we've got Buddy Bolden to thank for
so much. he filled the streets
with music and warmth for fourteen years. there's
only one photo of him and it's
pretty blurry. in the photo you also see
two clarinetists. one with a large
drooping mustache and one who's missing

his face. they're standing in front of something
that looks like tent-canvas gently stirring as if
a white horse were galloping behind it.

inside the tent it's snowing. it's cold
and the only warmth comes from a small
iron stove and Buddy Bolden's trumpet

3.

he blew too hard. everyone said that he
blew too hard. he's gonna blow
his brains out of his skull, they said. and that's
more or less what happened

it was right in the sunshine during
the Mardi Gras Parade in New Orleans 1907
and Mahogany Hall shone whiter than
ever with its windows full of naked
girls and ostrich feathers. Buddy Bolden
led all the bands in town along Canal Street

when he put the trumpet to his lips
to blow his signature tune Funky Butt
Funky Butt Take It Away there was sudden
complete silence. no sound came out
of the trumpet. the music drove backwards
up into his head and rushed around in his
brain like a berserk streetcar. he
kept blowing until people thought
the trumpet would uncoil when suddenly
something burst inside him

all the people stopped and looked at him
just as he collapsed on the street
without a sound. no sound could be heard in the whole town
the ambulance came gliding
slowly as in a dream without sirens
and the crowd parted to let it through.
they lifted Buddy Bolden up
and no one heard so much as a click
when the doors were closed behind him

4.

all the mirrors were cracked
at the mental hospital too. year after year. a long
crack straight across his face. sitting
on the edge of his bed in striped blue pajamas
he paints a big poster

> Buddy Bolden's
> Original Jass
> & Ragtime Band

a streetcar he says electric and crazy
in a light-blue New Orleans on the bottom of
the sea. silence. not even white bubbles
rising to the surface. not even a surface. in 1931 he
found his trumpet put it to his lips
and cracked all the windows in the streetcar
with a single note. the water rushed in
reason returning and then death
at 11 in the morning

Davenport Blues

Bix Beiderbecke (1903-1931)

1.

And I ride the Rock Island Line, westward from Chicago
where the water is freezing in hundreds of water towers,
black with grief over the rosy-cheeked trumpeter
drowned in the tear-flooded orchestra pit of the 20s.
Doors are slamming. A whistle blows.
I'm rolling backward through his life on heavy iron wheels,
                    Chicago-Davenport, and farther
                    back to the new world
                    where the vast cornfields wait
                    under frozen ground.

Past Illinois' rolling auto-graveyards, past
farm machines that are harvesting only snow
beneath enormous masses of cloud.
Rock Island Line, boxcar after boxcar, coach after coach
of figure-skating princesses asleep under coils of cigarette smoke.
                    Behind their closed blue eyelids
                    he is still on tour
                    with Bee Palmer, The Shimmy Queen,
                    riding through the twilight.

          Rock Island Line eastward to Chicago;
          his mournful musician's tuxedo,
          the cornet's ring, shinier than his patent-leather shoes,
          everything's sliding away on a saxophone arabesque
          where there is no ground beneath his feet
          for a long, long time.

2.

The old used record store on Tomtebo Street in Stockholm.
I'm 17 years old and in the stacks of 78s I come across
DAVENPORT BLUES, foxtrot, *Bix Beiderbecke & his Rhythm Jugglers,*
recorded January 26th, 1925 at the railroad station in Davenport
just as the train went by, the Rock Island Line
                that connects
                east to west
                then to now
                life to life.

Chorus after chorus of railroad cars through the store
where every detail comes out sharp.
The street outside already more diffuse,
people's fluttering shadow-play,
pencil gray, half erased
while the cars blindly grope their way along the curbs.
Davenport Blues, *Decca,* Beethoven's head in gold on the label
                and a scratch in the middle of the cornet solo
              scratch in the middle of the cornet solo.
        —Please lift the pickup!
But the matron behind the counter is hard of hearing, 2 kronor 75 öre
and Christmas wrapping paper far into May to slip the record into.
                A gleam of light across the grooves
                as across his hair
                combed slick with hair tonic.

3.

            A gleam of light
on the train wheel, 78 rpm through Davenport,
a city in outer space, winter streets
full of dead baseball dreams and college girls' giggles

smothered in scarves,
snowflakes syncopated into water droplets on the train window
into tears beneath the eyelids of the figure-skating princesses
                              the instant
                              his tuxedo's bow tie
                              starts flapping,
                              a black butterfly
                              over the ice.

          The rails, two parallel rivers of frozen steel.
At infinity they will meet where time meets time—1969, 1957,
1925 behind heavy train-window curtains where everything is black and
     white.
With jerky steps a woman walks through the flicker of silent film
to turn off a gramophone
whose needle is figure-skating across the record label
into Beethoven's gilded eye.
The music is sucked backward through the brass horn.
Cigarette ash across the shining grooves.
Snowfall over the fields in Iowa
where telephone poles stomp backwards in foxtrot rhythm.

The black butterfly lands again on his shirtfront
                              a frozen white field
                              full of the silence
                              left
                              by the story
                              I'll never tell... .

Bunk Johnson in New Iberia

The sunshine dries into dust
in the brown-red fragrance from the Tabasco factory.
The furrows in his face, decades of stubble fields,
the truck tires' dry rubber lips in a time that isn't his,
flaking like the plank wall that his shadow has pressed into.
Rusty springs force their way through the driver's seat,
his ribs press through his overalls.
A deep drag makes his cigarette butt glow.

He waits in the heat outside the Western Union office
waits for the teletype machine behind the roll-down shade
to start ticking: Come back sweet Papa.

Back to the beginning
when only the hundred thousand notes beyond the scale
are real.
Back to the city
where all roads began,
as the heart pumps blood
out into the arteries' ever finer system of passageways.
His face young again, reflected in the trumpet's brass
pressed against the lips that force his breath
through dark labyrinths
where the pistons go up and down inside the valves.
They shunt the air through a verdigrised maze
until it rushes out the bell note by note,
darkness given power to get sorrow moving
until all feet are tapping.

Back out onto the roads to a thousand towns
where the pulsebeat is the sledgehammer
that pounds tent pegs into the earth.

The circus tent still rises every night
to a height of 1,000 yards.
"Tiger Rag" tears loose from the trumpet
in a streaked salto mortale from trapeze to trapeze
by acrobats in patched tights
medallioned with constellations in brass.
When the drum roll breaks off they fall to the ground.
The fire-eater walks around the ring
swallowing gaslight after gaslight.
Later he sleeps calmly all night
with his head between the tiger's jaws.

Every dawn they move on
        and leave behind only
                an elephant turd as big as a soup bowl
                        on a deserted main street.

Until the labyrinth of roads grew narrower and narrower,
became tunnels through sunshine always more intense
and the dust whirled.
Amid the stubble fields the freight train's pistons slow down,
hiss air out into the landscape,
which trembles and disintegrates.
On the sign he reads NEW IBERIA.
It was the town all roads led to
and no roads led away

from the back yard where the dust eats the truck
that eats its way ever deeper into the dust
until after ten years
the roll-down shade snaps up at Western Union
and someone shouts:
Telegram from New Orleans to Mr. Johnson!
He gets up, takes the piece of paper and reads:
Please come back....

Winter Tour

Not to be where one is, and yet to be present
in time and space on a long tour through the snowdrifts
where one can sit in the band bus and drink beer
as frozen as the sap in the trunks of the pines,
and observe a moose on a snow-covered lake—
how it sniffs, turns and sort of veers off,
getting smaller, while its hooves kick up snow
and the white field grows. It returns
a few miles further on, in black silhouette
on a yellow triangle with a red border. That's the pine forest's pennant
and the shining lake of summer has shrunk to a traffic mirror
near a gas station where the cars stand still and drink.

In the evening the landscape we traveled through all day
gets measured on the bass drum and illuminated by a light bulb.
There's a lazy pulse coming from inside it,
beating in the stage floor, through my soles
and up through my body.
The band plays "Moose March" and I recite
"Back to the beginning
when only the hundred thousand notes beyond the scale
are real." After the reading
I go backstage while the music continues in the hall,
one, two, soon three cigarettes from here.

I stand amid folding tables and stacked-up chairs
and regard, beside the steel doors of the delivery dock,
a red sign SPRINKLER VALVE.
There's a dark smell of moose steak from the kitchen.
The cook is rattling pots and pans, her apron
is cut from the large field of snow.
Tomorrow I'll wake up in Room 301 at the main hotel

in Härnösand, open the window and breathe in the whiteness.
I can hear the bass player snoring a solo in the next room.
A single boat at the docks, *Ebba Victor.*
The snowplow makes mounds taller than people.
Things scrape against each other, steel on asphalt,
and almost inaudibly at the window, snow on glass.
After a long silence I can also perceive
the sound of snow on snow, and far from here

the sound of snow on your bare skin,
goose bumps rising at the buzz of the alarm clock.

from *Back to You*

1980

Star-goalie

Streams of light play over the ice,
　　the blue lines, red lines and circles.
The hockey rink's an enormous spaceship
　　　　of frozen light, driven by
　　the dark energy of countless human voices.
The goalie lowers his visor.
　　　　　　He's the pilot.
　　　　Inside glass booths
　　soundproof to the hum,
　　radio voices cry: Liftoff!

　　The spaceship rises above darkened stands
toward the ice-gods' galaxy.
　　　　　They thunder toward each other, gum-chewing jaws
　　　　　　brighter movements
　　　　　　quicker colors
　　across a planet of shining ice
　　　　　　　with a different law of gravity. Hockey stars
skating comets. Only in ice-light
　　　　　　can their colors sizzle.

　　　　His heavy goalie's suit
　　　　pulls him down toward the darkness of anti-stars
　　the dark oceans where spaceships founder.
In his memory slapped pucks echo through pine forest
　　beside an outdoor rink
　　　　and the stovepipe in the changing-shack
　　is glowing red. A thousand light years ago
he shot a frozen dog-turd through the light of streetlamps
　　　　　along the sidewalks' sanded crust of ice.

It's still flying.
Now he glides backward
   a gigantic crab
      going into his cage. His arms snap at the nets
      of another time.

   Broken
   above the crossroads of the universe,
  riveted there by winter stars—
his body. Jaw cracked
    eyes dull
  his heart pierced by a slap shot.

Behind his white death mask
   in rushing meltwater
     the ice gives birth again
       to the primordial land
      furrowed slabs of rock, granite polished clean.
   Light is transformed, becomes melting ice.
Here is where his colored suit will fall,
        his white face mask
    stare blindly
  upward.
 Sun will sparkle
pollen blow northward
     on a planet called the Earth.

   In another universe
   he will be resurrected
     as
   THE STAR-DIVER

The National Hospital, Oslo, September 1976

In the evening your face would light up
in the light from the page.
Now you're surrounded by white rectangles—
walls, sheets, doors.
Tubes carry blood and nutrients into your body
and urine out.
Half your body lies stiff,
has already left this room.

I ran in pouring rain through Oslo's streets,
into every hotel soaking wet:
My father is dying …
They said: Sorry.
We have no rooms.
Then I came here in wet clothes.

The nurse shouted into you:
Your son is here!
But behind your eyelids the dying had already come in
as soundlessly as the nurses through the door.
It drew you into your shell
like I used to withdraw into mine
when you wanted to have a word with me.
Your life was almost all fluid now,
running into you a drop at a time.
Air bubbles in the plastic tubes going into you
were like empty words
but your fingers drummed on my hand,
touched me.
You were back in the first language,
in wordlessness.

But the dream spoke with your voice.
You came to me in a suit of shadows and brown shoes,
slightly stooped, with a gray mustache.
You said: "I'm doing fine.
I'm still walking around here but live in another world,
much smaller than an atom.
I see each dust mote hugely magnified
and have so much to look at.
It contains all our knowledge.
For us who live here everything is large
and very clear.
When you've grown really little we'll meet here.
Here we know more than you know.
We know that dreams are a science
and hold everything you need to know.
Doctor Freud is here with me.
We have a psychoanalytic club
where we drink sweet German wines and smoke Doctor Freud's cigars
around long brown tables.
Every day we interpret the dreams we intercept from your world.
We can make out a pattern in them.
On Thursday we're having another meeting.
Then we'll see if we can help you.
So long for now. I'm leaving
but I won't close the door behind me."

Death begins early, one step at a time.
Is it as full of life
as life is of death?
Am I almost as much over there
as you are here?
The contours of two worlds fall through each other
and outside the sickroom window
the big chestnut tree beside the parking lot
rushes in the wind.

It is full of fruit.
The prickly green-gold husks are life.
The red-brown kernels death.
They hit the ground hard
and crack on the asphalt.

The chestnut's dark foliage rushes louder
than the sickroom's shiny death machines,
fluorescent tubes, water pipes.
Now the rushing in your bloodstream
is a language with only black words
from all the pages you've read.
And the sickroom door is a white rectangle
with no words left.
You open it
but it doesn't close behind you.

from *Gaslight*
1983

Blood Poisoning

Sink slowly into my own chambers
darker than the wards of Crown Princess Lovisa's Children's Hospital
where I've been in bed for thirty years.
The skin has been peeled from my body, layer by layer.
All the internal organs colored on a medical plate.
The wrist swollen. A dark line starts there,
pulses through the vein, across the armpit, toward the heart.

In one room sits Crown Princess Lovisa in violet beauty,
a playing-card queen.
She's crocheting, crocheting new blood vessels for the children,
loop after loop of red blood vessels for the children.
—Patience, mon cher,
she whispers into a speaking tube that ends at my bedside.
Patience.
The card game fans out on the blanket,
a swarm of red hearts.
Toward them too the poisoning starts creeping.
       I'm drifting away
       along the blue canals
       that are my circulation.

The reflections of the hospital lamps make the marble floors more
    transparent than air.
Among the bone china on the rattling iron carts
the biscuits dance sadly
because she isn't coming
because no one is coming
because nothing here shines more intensely than absence.

Laid to rest between stiff winter sheets, I burn
in a fever-summer of canals bluer than Nirvana, where canoes are gliding.
Clover, I think, from clubs to clovers.
They too bestow a certain happiness
if there are lots of them and they blossom white, veined with red blood.
Close up. Only close up,
but here everything is far away.
The summer a black suit in a card game.
The poisoning a whisper in my blood.
Everything's far away outside the dark room
where only the crack around the door is drawn in light.

The sick children's castle sinks through the darkness.
The clock strikes in the Church of Queen Ulrika Eleonora,
as heavily as the heart in its tower of flesh.

Patience

The sound of the needle crocheting, crocheting
on the other side of the door.
Her room is a rectangle of light.
With a sigh she snuffs out the lamp
and all of Stockholm lights up in her window.

Above the square at Fridehemsplan the cinema's enormous Dragon burns,
twisted into glass veins where the beauty of the evening becomes neon.
Underneath it in the red velvet cave, the children's pale faces.
Light-rays from their feverish eyes project onto the wall
fairy tales made of neon, of fire, of flickering celluloid
until the rectangle of light before them becomes a room inside them,
a gold miner's cabin teetering above the abyss.
The top of the bowler hat covered with snow.
The gold is burning ice-cold in the stove.

All that gives warmth is the fever.
The Dragon moves its luminous tongue
                              whispering.

Persephone

Silence, built of bricks from old tenements,
glued on with every layer of wallpaper
where spring is pressed into darkening floral patterns.
She opens the drapes and a feeble light describes
all these states of the soul, highly nuanced and distinct
but so sad that they lack names of their own.
Streaks of light so broad that her thoughts can walk on them
out above the roofs where the wind is tossing the pigeons around, light
so distant that it can't remember its source,
and now it finally sinks to the ground
through the sun-panels on the linoleum.

So many words about the light—it's so sparse here
that it occupies every thought, describes
her limbs pulled from his greatcoat like potato sprouts.
The whole of her fights against him, she scratches with her nails
at where his eyes must be, wrestles with him
inside the dark coat, his grip doesn't loosen, bends
her in toward him until her joints crack.
The kick to the groin
and she thinks she's free
when his shadow covers her again
plants its foot on her throat
and receives her curses for the thousandth time.

Until now she has endured the motions of love
as if the only way out of his musty smell and clothes
were through him.
His skeleton a set of stakes around her
and the budgie hanging by one foot from the roof of its cage,
imitating his voice.

The dawn comes on more slowly each day.
Her silence is the geraniums,
pink mouths that breathe against the windowpane, misted
like the cheese-clock on the breakfast table.
The dark jacket sleeve keys open the cover of a flat tin.
Oil oozes from the sardine's silver body
when he holds it up on his fork.

She stands behind him in stockinged feet,
inwardly cries herself toward the sea
where the foam calcifies to shells
twisted around lustrous interiors;
to olive groves where tables are set only with knives
and he staggers backward down to the waves, bellowing,
with blood gushing from his belly.

What music has frozen into this building?
A dense symphony with no other consolation
than what can be extracted from the steady presence of the walls
and from the knowledge that everything built of light
is condemned to remain invisible.
Her lips move at the memory
of another breathing, deeper inside her,
so close to her ear. And it is just now,
it is long, long ago
and so early that morning is still throbbing under her skin,
various gradations of softness, so early
that every pore inhales the summer city
where the cab drivers are still asleep in their cars.
Breathing under heavy bridge-vaults, slipping bright water
reflected in a window, a silken square.

Her lips are drawn toward the glass
as if one person's sorrow
could add something to the common human sadness—

an architecture of stiffened phrases;
as if billowing grayness weren't enough, the sea
a damp membrane under her eyelids.
She utters something indifferent
into the room behind her
but her voice is still trembling.

She stands completely still at the window,
blurred by the seasons' quick changes
like the face in a passing commuter train.
On the inner surface of her eyes, tiny cityscapes, all dreamt out;
her belly domed, the skin so thin that we can see
the bearded dwarf inside,
with its head downward,
that will be born into the convex cities observed
through the drinking glasses at sidewalk cafés.

He will carry her like eczema in his memory.
Alone in an entranceway he'll be struck by the thought
of the light that stayed on in the stairwell, automatically,
for a minute after she went out through the doors.

Åkersbodarna, July 1981

Like children the trees carry their souls
out in the open, strong in their power
to stand motionless and listen to the rushing from deep inside.
The girls' laughter and the dog's white tail-tip, patches of sun
in the leaf-shade where the Toyota stands with doors open,
a cast metal version of the facet-eyed bugs
that set the summer humming in the grass.

After rain, gravity gradually weakens
as the mysteries are cleared up once more.
That strong smell: pineroot.
That acrid smell: spruce resin.
And the one who's only a year old
is holding his empty bottle.
Dried in the bottom, a half-moon of milk.
His eyes blue with astonishment
as if he'd just landed this morning on this strange planet.
He lay down beside these aliens
and they were united in his sleep.

It's all the years, they fill the air
with earth-smell, leaf-smell, steaming from stones and wet crevices,
they flash from glinting tin roofs, drip from branches
and get under my shirt
so that I will remember and record
what falls backwards through all my senses
while my eye tries to catch what's vanishing.

The light is so strong that everything is X-rayed
yet still cool,
displays only what the night already knew
in the shadow of the palm against your body,

soft shining in the dark that was my darkness
until it became the language of fingertips and lips,
of the trees the rain fell through so they rustled
as when an eyelash lowers very close up
in a completely silent room.

You lie stretched out on the grass, your hip an arched hillock
while your heavy breasts multiply into bocci balls,
a colorful planetarium on the ground.
I give them the same names
as Saturn's newly discovered moons:
Dione, Titan, Thetys,
a rain-shimmering moonstone,
Mimas with only one crater, a lonely breast in space
where the grasshopper lands and shrills
until everything's vibrating, more fragile
than the summer after a war.

Créole

A migratory flight west from Gibraltar
to nowhere,
Atlantis.
They will never return.
Where the ocean ends they follow the caravels
out into the billowing Sargasso of the starry skies,
prairies of rocking salt water
where all boundaries dissolve, land becomes water, water
land, floating islands, ocean depths where fat eels are born
and new worlds beyond the end of this one.

Nearsighted after reading too long in the dark,
I turn the pages of a book where no text is visible.
How intensely the light shines from them.
A flying fish swims through the air above my head.
A thousand window shutters stripe the sunlight.
I'm travelin' light.
Almost no baggage:
a pair of jeans, some T-shirts
and the huge erasure Europe has left in my brain.
I'm traveling light.
I am light, traveling.

—M'sieu! M'sieu!
From between her thighs the Creole woman has given birth
to the market's mounds of fruits and spices:
pomegranates, cinnamon bark, pimentos, limes,
pineapples fertilized by the sun.
The sea rolls backward, swell after swell,
gleaming teeth, rocking muscles slippery with sweat, giving birth

to island after island, clouds of greenery capping the hills.
A stone moves: a tortoise! Crabs clatter sideways
conquistadors with enormous iron prostheses.

Over and over the French admiral comes ashore,
eyelids: heavy cannon-ports under the white plume.
Picket after picket of sugarcane,
hollow bones crunching in the hand-turned mills,
the watermelon's huge heart is split
and the earth is greasy with blood
pounding underfoot.
All the documents penned to pieces by the damp;
rotting flakes of parchment, ink that has run,
charts of drifting archipelagos.
The only true account: the neck shackles
and the rusty cannon above the mouth of the harbor.

I walk through colors as strong as the smells
from the restaurants' garbage piles.
Crab cadavers, an army that came ashore
with their shields on their heads, crushed
in the sun-stench of mass graves.
Flies around the wise lips of the fish-heads,
the grinning face of an Indian god
arisen from the deep
and every night Orion deeper upwards,
a membrane of salt over blind eyes.
The whole sky is held in the coconuts' heavy testicles,
unborn, dimly painted with death-milk
in the night where the Arawak children are keening,
stunted small as frogs by hunger for their mothers' breasts,
in the night where the slaves cast themselves into the sea

to drown
so they could be born
back to Africa.

The Creoles sit astride their drums and fly away.
Their smiles more secret than the Europeans' bank accounts.
All night the vibrating whistle of the bamboo flutes.
The crickets' shrill ringing
from a lost continent—
Africa.
Atlantis.
Europe.

(Martinique, 15 November – 15 December 1981)

History-painting

1.

The typewriter at the evening window
dreams my fingertips
across the keys, blue shirtsleeves, clouds of cigarette smoke,
dreams my thoughts through itself.
The ribbon rolls black through year after year.
Hard metal in relief hammers time into signs.

Darker down through the years …
As if I were seeing it for the first time …
Beckomberga 1945. The Assistant Doctor's residence inside the gates.
The huge metal garbage bin half buried in the ground.
For a whole afternoon I stood at the bottom of the bin and screamed
until suddenly a face turned up in the circle,
pale-gray skin, watery eyes, hospital clothes.
His hand reached down and pulled me up into the light.
That was my birth.

The same hand, many years later,
reached out toward me at the mental hospital.
He was sitting at a table and painting his dreams.
The watercolor brush in the jar turned the water pink.
"In the dream's room," he said, "there are only three walls
that are part of the dream.
The fourth wall, where you are, is not part of the spirit world.
I realized this in a dream.
My beloved came toward me from the foot of the bed.
Where my head was she stopped
and looked at me, sort of questioning.
She was trying to explain to me
that this fourth wall is an abyss."

But that time, at my birth, I was five years old and stared into the light
from the gas stove's iron rings, wrought-iron flutes bent into circles
where the gas hissed out fire-dances from blue to orange
until the rough hunks of rock went rumbling around the pot.
The ring of fire was reflected in the kitchen window
above flesh-colored hospital dorms
where the mentally ill were embalmed by afternoon light
in bed after bed.
Their faces pale, without any features,
just their mouths on the pillowcases,
black holes from which their howling issued—
wordless gas.

2.

The train slows into Ljungskile Station.
Dark green curtains flutter in their leather tiebacks
until finally the station stops in the window with a judder.
I am still in a child's body
next to the heavy suitcase on the platform,
small hands and feet, but head disproportionately large
with an idiot's wise eyes that see the stationmaster and the trees
standing silent as the gnomon on a sundial.
Through the taxi window
glitter the millions of sun-flashes that are Ljungskile Bay
where the cows' silhouettes are wading at the water's edge.
Around their eyes and tails—flies in black armor flashing blue
like the fenders on the old Volvo
that drove me from the station to Ekeberg,
from a yellow house to a white one.

Within the walls of that small house, enormous furniture
in which the reflections darken into mahogany shadows,
chairs with lions' feet ready to leap

back to the manor-houses' bright drawing rooms
where they once …

The large trunk in the attic contains the past—
a Sunday suit, a letter,
a green postcard album with brass fittings—
all that's left of Uncle Arthur
who was driven insane "by love."
Gaudy greeting cards with gold lettering
where he comes whistling on his bike
wearing damask and his Sunday suit.
Straw hat on his head, bouquet of roses in his hand.
A brown-haired woman smiles at him from a window.
The battle of Lützen on tinted picture postcards.
His head has fallen to one side.
His left arm hangs limp under his cavalry soldier's armor,
gleaming horse-muscles, the grooms' cracking pistol-shots.
All the light plunges toward his body at the picture's center,
rushes toward a point inside him.
As he falls he clutches desperately at the horse
but the white body slips away between his hands
hooves raining down till they're stuck
among cinnamon-colored fern leaves.

The letter written in pencil: "A station waiting room, 19 Oct. 1910.
My dearest friend Arthur!
If you could know with what a heavy heart I write these lines.
Because they are the last ones to You dear friend …
I hope you will forget me
and not be too despondent …
Your one true friend
                    Natalia."

3.

Time a leaky faucet, second by second the whole night
drips down into the washbasin.
The thin, cool film bursts against the enamel.
The dripping has merged with the rushing in the trees' feather dresses
                    which streams in through the open window
                    held still by a white window latch
                    in the July night.

Everything streams back to the silent railway station.
The suitcase lonely in its shadow on the sunny platform.
The train starts rolling.
A brown-haired woman between fluttering compartment curtains.
A waiting room, heavy vaults of stone, three walls.
The fourth is not part of the dream.
The fourth is where you are.

Hammer letters through the ribbon's fabric
like sentences from the mouths of dead kings in Riddarholm Church,
drained of blood while wearing powdered wigs, or shot through the
    stomach
under horse-hooves, horse-hooves, horse-hooves
that hammer letter after letter
between Germany's November-frozen rabbit holes,
or with gummy rolls expanding in their bellies
so the sweat breaks out
through every pore in the heavy marble sarcophagi.

The 6th of November, 1632. Horse-hooves trampling his heart …

The 16th of March, 1792. The masked murderer's bullet …

The 19th of October, 1910. A waiting room …

On the flags of the conquered, eagles and fragments of letters decompose.
The run-over crow flattened into an emblem for those
                         who didn't understand
                         that everything that wants to live
                         eats life,
                         who didn't understand
                         that the cry of the seagull
                         is hoarse with raw fish,
                         that the crow's cadaver
                         in its wet overcoat
                         kindles the iris's light.

4.

Only the light of summer night is itself
above the paper where shadow after shadow from the past
lives my life toward me in the formal gardens of the old postcard-album.
Silent summer roads under dark masses of foliage
where some people are marble, some pillars of wood.
The goddess of love is also made of stone,
her temples and fingers.
You can break them off, small stumps of chalk
in the dream's eternal classroom
with which a still-living hand searches on the blackboard
for the conjugations of love. She flies among the tree trunks.
                       When his thoughts graze her skin
                       she screams greenery
                       from the roots of her hair, fingertips, throat

and she is once again the tree-branches' twisted dreams
outside the long hospital dorms, the pink ones,
petrified pieces of flesh joined to make walls and wards.

Wind through the branches that were her hands and shoulders,
wind writes among the leaves
word upon word that one can live in
>   as in madness
>   in another summer
>   where one wants to live.

Everything wants to return to its origin
before it was molded by his thoughts.
In the green whispers of the dense masses of foliage, there she is.
His presence is already playing over her groin,
ignites blond hairs on her raised arm
until her nakedness is a smile,
a gown of light, invisibly
moved by the wind,
which will open the heavy folds for him.

She spreads her thighs and exposes the hairy cleft.
He screams in horror.

5.

The darkness from inside me turns the large spools,
black dream-ribbons between me and the sheets of paper
and I am back in the deserted waiting room
where she is sitting in a dress made of shiny fabric.
So lonely, her hands folded one on the other,
so white, the pylons' insulators in the shunting yard of the dream.
The shadows of the trains pass by the window, surging like the shore
where the cows are chewing on the summer, an enormous Gobelin tapestry
that blackens into meat.

Only what you've lost is you,
visible for just a second when she smooths
her long hair away from her face.
Her lips and breast so close to me in the waiting room,
for just a moment, and I will always miss her.
Soundless switching of the heavy locomotives
destined for places that have sunk so deep in me
that they've taken on the color of my darkness.
Banisters coil upwards
through the stairwell's whiff of gramophone music
back to the kitchen, silent except for the hissing of the gas.

How translucent she is, in the open door's panel of light
with her hands at her sides
as at a fluoroscope exam.
Outside it's October
with maple leaves so red they stick to people's clothing.
The doorway so full of light in her wake
                    that I can go through it
                    out of the dream
                    still in her fragrance
                    still with her skin
                    around my own.

6.

These are the men who keep the night watch.
They have come to open a red gate in his brain.
We are in the house of dead opera arias
where everyone is finally disguised as himself.
His skin has been pulled down over my forehead.
Thus are we patched together with pieces from other people
and nonetheless remain in our own loneliness.
Each second enclosed

in the crystal chandeliers' glittering teardrops, falling,
a thin membrane between darkness and the light of madness
where all images are enlarged in the flames' hissing spangle of colors.

With flashing scissors of light the well-manicured hand
cuts the last threads that connect his brain to the universe.
Through the murmur of voices she comes toward him
naked behind closed eyelids.
He sees her filling with rot, her lips first.
                    Then her womb bleeds
                    through the thin papery skin.
                    He sees her again, black
                    on long bony legs,
                    a wading bird.
                    Between her feet
                    the moon-mice spring up, silver-gray, howling.

When the music falls silent he staggers over, gracefully,
in a final dance step, grabs hold of the tablecloth.
The glasses fall over. Deep inside the crystal,
                    his mirrored face,
                    flattened into a death mask,
                    creeps out in a runnel of blood
                    black
                    as typewriter letters.

Then she opens the blood-red gate and between
walls pulsing with flesh he rushes
back to his birth
until the fourth wall closes behind him.
The gardens lie deserted, pathways lined with beehives buried in snow
row after row
of wax cabinets
filled with the summer's dead voices:
Because they are the last ones to You dear friend…

7.

Yellow clouds, blue-gray clouds and silence are reflected in Ljungskile Bay.
The swimmers' laughs over at the Lyckorna Baths
and the old submarine, painted white, a breakwater
with its belly full of slimy stones
that have anchored it to the sandy bottom since 1918.
Tonight I could row a boat straight through my thoughts
reflected in pale water.

Bicycles roll through the summer evening,
whirring light from the darkness of their generators.
Trailers white with moonlight through the darkness of the leafy trees
where a bronzed woman
wriggles out of a flowered summer dress.
Soundlessly fabric falls to the ground.
Lit up by the roar of the propane stove, her body and his.

> Was their only way
> to the center of the world
> to sink into each other?
> Were the ropes that bound them
> their own blood vessels?
> The ragged bush
> between her thighs
> a blackthorn bush, ablaze
> with white flowers?

Their naked bodies, stiffened into statues,
breathe the moonlight back out through marble pores,
breathe back the sarcophagi's light
the hospital wards'
the waiting rooms' light.
Growing light among the orbiting worlds.
Light saw her.
That's how she became the light's visible body.

Light was inside her
came only
from her.
The moon's scream
more and more intense
screams her
back…

The black-flashing spools revolve
and transform letter after letter into darkness.
Words are hammered to death against typing paper
while I watch what continually dies
grow leaf after leaf
for the night's feather dress,
an enormous bird with outspread legs and wings.
Its head crowned with a crown of flaming constellations
                        hissing blue
                        galaxies of blazing gas
                        spiraling
                        spiraling
                        in a rising silent shriek.

from *The Star-diver*

1987

The Star-diver

1.

How many people are you, really? How many
am I? All I know is,
there are fewer of me all the time. So many shut their lips
when they noticed the space around them was expanding,
until silence was no longer imposed, but habitual.
Those who are left wear thicker and thicker overcoats
to keep out the cold from the others' silence
and the knowledge that their own growth
has caused others to wither away

                                        in silent institutions
where the hands of strangers have built a roof above them
tile by tile; where visits are rare
and never intended to give pleasure.
Now the coffee spoon starts to rattle in the cup
where the sugar cube never wants to dissolve and just gets
squarer. The unbuilt house already exists
in blue lines sketched out in the air. You lived in that house.
I know, I know—and I know too
that each day is a new jigsaw piece in the great puzzle
that can never come together even though
every piece fits all the others. More mute fingers
are always arriving and the composition grows
into something immeasurable and perpetually changing
that has been given the provisional name
Star-chart of lost opportunities

and I can only accept that it will grow larger
than any reality I know and control.
I go out through the door without saying goodbye,

since I have to pretend it's not for the last time.
And (later) out in the street, when I have the enormous structure
behind me, the windows are all filled with tiny waving hands.
They return whenever I doze off, under lowered lids they draw with their
    nails
on my retina: lines to guide me further in.
It's time. They point the way
beyond the coma of dependencies

where the motions keep getting violently closer to disorder
and all gravitation ceases in the emptiness left by steadily more indifferent
    words,
which is never the same: an infinite series of silences, all of them endless.
Void after void grows and changes.
Inside them beat the hearts
that are stronger than ours.

2.

I'm talking about dismantling.
You can cut wherever you please, it will still be a window
with your name written backwards across the whole view.
Buildings fold up like books.
They clap shut and no one has time to go through them again.
So much else is coming into the picture,
so much dust is falling on the roofs of old elevators
from a future you can already button yourself up in,

a jacket handed down to you, and dirty. It gives you free admission
to a library bombed in the blitz, where every morning
the caretaker unlocks the doors *as if nothing has happened.*
Hands touch the broken spines of books to heal them,
a dusting of lightning on their fingertips, and the pallor of these volumes

comes not from inside them but from the sky
which has crashed down through the ceiling.

Has the project ended, have its expectations collapsed,
or have they been transformed into remnants of us?
There are any number of ways out now that the walls have fallen,
liberation so complete that it's become a new imprisonment.
But more important than these transitions to a more transparent life
is what wells up from the seams between the systems of thought
we believe ourselves to be. No, I never understood them.
They were buildings I just visited by accident
like this library with its eternally bald caretaker,
annoyed at not being able to show his annoyance.
The registry is filled up with signatures. We're here somewhere
under all these names; we're searching for a way back
in total amnesia.

Nights are not the shadows of the days, coupled to each other
like freight cars. They are one, are one, are one.
All the truths melt back into one, shiny as a car key,
even though the crystal chandelier lies scattered across the floor.
It is the time of year called night.

3.

Perhaps the most important thing of all is waiting,
the time between two stereotyped events
which must be killed though no one knows with what weapon.

The door is white. The door is closed. Very white but closed.
Here's an armchair.
Piles of newspapers already read by those who were here yesterday.
All that's left is a flight

through the Persian carpet's imitation angst:
to fall asleep breathing slowly, each breath neatly ironed and in black and
    white checks,
to disappear in the discreet smell of sweat from your shirt,
to become something "repressed,"
something that has prevented someone from developing,
an outgrown set of clothes on the other side of the round window,
tumbling around in pre-shrunk choreography
until it becomes part of the rotation of the centrifuge
whose forces are greatest at the periphery,
far from the centers where truths are compressed into dark matter
and the draperies hang in folds of marble.

Only then will you find what's happening around you growing clear
when you take a few steps out into the city, which on a day like today
belongs to everyone, an overcoat of thin gray cloth.
In the space between your outstretched arm and your body
raindrops splash up a few millimeters after they hit,
a bright spray above the street—
a thousand tiny sculptures carved in water, you are shattered
into an anthology of rushing noise, so lacking sense that only someone
whose attention wanders aimless and disconnected
can apprehend it

                    and see that each day has its own composition
hard enough to discern so it suits everyone,
compounded of a million details that are not intended
to live in any harmony but the one created by indifference,
a swarm of disparities that aren't even contrasts,
that just exist simultaneously without arousing much interest.
A row of hats on an escalator to nowhere
on a perfectly empty afternoon
with a whiff of pomade around your sweatband.
Your shirt flutters on a line until the wind has drunk it dry
and only the smell of the water remains.

Only the basics endure:
height: 5 foot 7 (without shoes); eyes: blue; hair: dark blond.
Nothing else. Just that.

To arrive at nothing is no reason for disappointment
if arriving at something was never one's purpose.

(fragment of an epilogue)

When you and everything you're familiar with
have been dispersed by the rushing traffic, your stand-ins
will take over the pedestrians' shadows,
flapping in closets shaken by a storm.
They are waiting for their voices, with their tongues they grope
for words that lie so deep in the mind
they seem to come from nowhere.
I remain in the gap between us and now—
dancing stars, dancing stars—and I am not there.
To arrive at nothing…. And nonetheless the disappointment
is grounds for a new beginning, and nonetheless
the beginning is grounds for new disappointment, and nonetheless
the grounds are what one didn't mean to arrive at
and didn't arrive at, either—dancing stars.

The Gate Coin

The days don't get lost, we get lost in them,
sweaty pennies in a fist that hits and hits.
Whose breeches fart in your face?
Whose nosebleeds and wild strawberries pour onto the sand?
We ask as if we've already forgotten the dead children,
but they're so close that they can almost, but only almost
speak to us without complaining,
for we have not abandoned them.

The gate is still standing open against the horizon
where horse and wagon become dust that settles
over knees and elbows bent on mattresses
that have been stuffed with straw and hundred-krona bills.
Face after face, framed in brown wood,
care-worn and flyblown in more and more old-fashioned shaving mirrors
while we hurry on through forests of greeting cards,
the dead wishing each other a peaceful Christmas in faded ink
or merry Easter landscapes where a chicken with a parasol
and another in a top hat pedal by on tricycles
so that we will know that death
is not the inevitable end of everything.
Tapping can already be heard from inside the beautifully painted eggs,
and daffodils and narcissi blossom again
when the spring sun's dress falls to the ground
and the wagon rolls over it.

In compensation something else must disappear.
This year it was the rabbits,
a round hole in the wire cage that's been cut with shears,
and inside nothing but some small, hard rabbit turds
and a plate full of grass.
It was the stray rabbits

that set the dark grass in motion tonight,
and tomorrow night they'll be buried in a plastic bag
in the animal-damp darkness.
The children mourn this more than their own death,
which rolls through the dust almost unnoticeably,
almost totally unnoticed rolls through the dust,
almost totally unnoticed.

Adonais

The tower leans forward, a watchman
over all this rain from the Renaissance
this spring-winter when everyone's talking about escape routes
and the buses surge forward through the masses of water.
This month when everyone's talking about bombs.
The pant-legs cold and wet against the shins.
This is the site of the house where Shelley lived.
There is no roof on the house where Shelley lived.
There are only thorny bushes and broken glass
in the house where Shelley lived.
The walls were lit up for a moment, no longer.

Hamlets are in many ways more "eternal" than cities,
are constantly renewed, but on the same old patterns
determined by some ancient marble statue, buried and forgotten.
There is a farmhouse in pink cement
with two soaked hens scratching around, there is
one naked knee peeking out from a river of tar,
the dream of falling asleep and waking up inside a woman.
I pray your shoulders toward the horizon, I pray
your blood back into the fields, I pray
the lightning blue in the riverbed,
a triangle of wet flowers.

It is impossible to be one with the landscape
unless you float out into the filthy water.
Hotel Eden is dozing behind its window shutters.
In bored rows the bottles wait for the tourists
this spring-winter when everyone's talking about poisoned wine.
It's harder and harder to keep track of
which year is blowing by outside.
The only guest has cotton-balls in his ears.

Over and over he tries to touch the waitress's breasts.
The umbrella blows inside out.
The palms on the boardwalk blow inside out.
Green are the waves that come rolling in.
The one thing I ask of you: give me your life, only that.

(Pisa—Viareggio, April 1986)

Für Elise

Not driving nails into the piano is the issue,
not setting fire to the curtains.
It's not a question of freedom from your upbringing
but an upbringing for a freedom that exists
only occasionally. Not to take on
the stiffened expressions in the family portrait above the piano,
the ones that make the notes go sour
when unpracticed fingers search for her,
stumbling across the keyboard.
To sit in a chair that's altogether too big
and read the encyclopedia volume by volume
until the entire known world
trickles into you in alphabetical order
and then to re-create it with an erector set perforated by small holes
through which freedom passes as through a strainer.
To be slowly filled by it
as the flowerbed is filled by the water from the pipe
until it's flooded or a pink geranium finds its way up.

Guarding the Air

1.

Take a feather, dip it in ink and draw a swallow.
It will be a swallow that's missing one feather,
just the one that would enable it to fly.
You must try something else.
Repeat the words "wide of the mark by harking the lark"
so many times that they become the only truth about you.
Now your thoughts can climb high above the city like a swallow.
They leave a long trail behind them in the air
by means of which you can follow their course.
When you've finished thinking, this line is erased
but so high up that almost no one will notice.

Fluttering, yes, but who's without a flutter
in his delivery, or nearing delivery?
The swallow sleeps through a wing-beat that lasts an hour.
For today only, the factory chimneys have been taken down,
brick by brick, but the columns of smoke are left standing against the sky,
just as sun-dazed lovemaking leaves behind
a pearl of semen on a leaf, the print of grass on a white rump.
Trees and chimneys aren't more real than humans.
They merely breathe more slowly and remain in themselves
longer, but they fall harder when they fall,
with a crash as brutal as the words the comics use
to describe how a hard fist meets a soft jaw.
But they don't cry, or not in any way we can fathom
as we lie stretching out in the grass.

2.

So many search for the perfect imitation of a kiss,
search for themselves in dark corners,
not here in the sunshine
where you can follow anyone at all
and when he turns around, suddenly see yourself.
Things aren't always that simple, but not
that complicated either. So many veer off,
deny all knowledge, even of well-known
squares and monuments, adopt impersonal speech
in which they themselves are diluted and scattered,
just as a thermos always gets smashed on a school outing
and sparkling slivers in bluish-gray hot chocolate
trickle into the ground. That's how face after face disappears—
glitter can go lifeless even in the sun (Eurydice)—
and is nowhere to be found, was nowhere to be found,
not today, not tomorrow,
will never be found.

Where is the dancer apart from the dance, and where are those
brave enough to build monuments not of bronze but of air,
as permanent as the eternal going by and being gone?
Where are those who dare to be transformed into themselves in this?
There are years in which no one seems to be left,
when you get a dial tone in the middle of a conversation
and the last thing you heard was an unfinished opinion
like "'excessively scholarly'—ha ha!"
or the fire alarm in the all too fashionable hotel,
which would start to wail whenever the chef flambéed some filet mignon,
a saxophone set off by too much heat
and no one playing it.

Only a sick five-year-old can teach us to disappear
in earnest and with courage, yes, almost with a smile. He says:

"You can never die if you have your hat on." No, never,
and if you're holding the string of a kite you can never die.
The horizon is so low that the sky almost seems to be everything.
The threads that keep it from leaving the earth
invisible in the clear air.
I dedicate this day to those who must move on,
who won't manage to stay here tomorrow.

The boy on the swing smears out into air,
collects in his outline again for a second before
the pendulum motion takes him back through himself.
Five fingers can slip into a glove.
Are there tunnels in the air to disappear through?
In a place like this you can suddenly smell
cigarette smoke, but no one's there.

3.

Is it just something I've imagined?
No, when I was five years old there were coloring books
that you didn't need any colors for.
All you had to do was dip your brush in water
and draw it across the pages.
Soon landscapes in full color appeared
and now I am back in them, a few minutes after the sun-shower
that's made the street and the lawn a little cooler, a little darker.

Just add water and your soul becomes visible again
in the bodies and objects around you—large, young and inconceivable,
and clear-sighted rather in the way of five-year-olds, observant as they are
of unavoidable sliding toward simplification
and elucidation, of turns so sharp
that they can cut a per-
son into two, like jacket lapels.

In spite of this you get the impression of an almost merciless logic,
since the shifts aren't visible to the naked eye.
All the pictures of them turn out to be images of a standstill,
but comparison tells its unmistakable tale:
a foot is on its way from one room into another, which is the same room.
The key word is change, and it too gradually changes
on sunny sidewalks, in front of shops closed for the summer, and farther
    along.

Each time I look at the clock-hands they've taken new positions.
In between they've run around like madmen.
The heat presses down onto the streets, a swarm of colored dots
slightly out of register in the Sunday supplements
where a red mouth in the middle of a cheek smiles at a double cup.

The apartment houses turn inside out.
Empty back yards quiver with voices, frying smells, the clatter
of cooking paraphernalia, and *Red Sails in the Sunset,* a hit
left behind from some other summer in a radio
that hasn't been used for a while. There are still women,
yes, there are still women in salmon-pink underwear
smoking Ritz extra-longs and sunning the soles of their feet on the
    windowsills.
Or are they just pictures in my mind, brought to life by the heat
and now being slowly exposed until they're invisible again
above the peaks of the roofs?

If you can talk about peaked roofs here.
The houses are just chopped off when they get high enough.
There are restrictions on how much blue each building
can occupy; but whatever is left belongs to our senses.
Every one of us has mineral rights there, we carry the claim with us like
    an LP

along the streets' unbending extension into summer heat
where the tune playing now brings with it all earlier ones.
It also hints at the part of the melody that hasn't been played yet
but is already causing a slight delay in our movements
until everything happens at the same tempo,
the same dumb tempo, listless but overpowering.
We do not think, yet we are.
We think, yet we do not exist.

4.

Here is the land that never, is the land that never,
the land that becomes. Here are we who become more and more unclear
because our visibility was rushed and fraudulent.
Do you still love me? Smoke grows stale in coils above our shoulders,
the answer is a timid smile. The answer to such questions
is a smile one can vanish in and still remain outside of.
A and B are cycling around a lake.
A travels at a speed of 8 km/hr,
B at a speed of 11 km/hr.
The lake is infinitely large.
Where will they meet?

Words pump the air.
The cyclist, going uphill now, pumps faster
because the air is hissing out of his tires.
How long will it take? How long
will it take you to think everything that's yours to think
and what will be left to think then? There will be nothing
to think then and you will be filled with a deep serenity.
Clothed in total silence you will be able to observe
how the pebbles crack like swallow's eggs, but they crack without a sound

and you understand the silence that pours out from inside them
as *content,* a content you recognize from yourself
and you can never again lose your way, no, never again lose your way.

There you sit. Yes, here we sit, are you still there?
Yes, we are still here and this landscape will be with us forever.
It will carry us along with it as one season turns to the next
like the pages of a coffee-table book.
The boys playing rounders are flipped jerkily across the grass in faded
    colors.
The ball got lost a decade ago
but the free laps never stop, no never,
as long as the swallow is fluttering up there.

from *My Winterland*

1990

Decayed

A dog's bark from outside the invariability, and weeks of innocence
are replaced by gray rain. Everything catches in the dog's coat,
rain mixed with gravel comes into the house. It is every day.
The frost sits where it sits. Sunk into the mess,
a catafalque or a bureau drawer? In today's situation,
it's all the same: a similarity becomes a difference,
a difference a similarity, and the corpses of both
decompose into shreds here, a sediment hard to describe.

In the mountain's pockets the inscrutable ones are sleeping, all
in different positions. Each one has his own shelter,
just slightly roomier than overalls.
They carry the mountain, not inside themselves, they carry it
literally on their foreheads. Through them it acquires
its thoughtful appearance. Yet that is only
a poster pasted over something else. The ocean?
Someday that too will be torn away, or papered over again.
The rolls of wallpaper stand ready behind warehouse doors.
An unmistakable odor of glue takes over the hollow chambers.
Are the shafts leading back closed off, their entrance
entrancing no one, not household
words but household thoughts, packaged in dark wrapping paper
dispatched inward so it can open *us* under the dome?
The door slammed shut behind itself,
locked out on both sides of

In the beginning, and now we are back there.
It wriggles its way out of here without wriggling us out.
What keeps piling up is still probabilities,
circuit-breakers capable of changing the lighting
on something that recalls a hunting scene:

someone leans over something heavy and collapsed.
The shadow of an evergreen forest blows roughly through an eyebrow
furrowed in the discontent produced by killing.

That's how the raincoats of the years will be turncoats,
the dog's row of teeth gnaw something white.
Slag will accumulate, and ruggedness,
water will rust toward the horizon, water pipes
eat their way into the weeks
and empty them.

The Night Wanderer

We are here to try to expose a lightness
that is murder's lightness, which spatters dresses and blouses
darkly, insolubly. And since it has rained
heat hangs under the trees, muggy with radio voices.
The pastel colors of the scooped ice cream eagerly match
the frozen flavors they're designed to represent,
but also match the colors of the flats
that are raised on the park stage for God knows which popular comedy.
Something reminiscent of *The Night Wanderer*
but in brilliant sunlight that makes our own colors too
resound almost madrigally.

What we knew slips away and slips away again
along the inner-city streets, footsteps visible only in the fog
and now it has lifted. Here there is room again to think
about everything we've possessed unjustly yet still want to keep.
But why think about it now? The parking meters can
ponder that under their silver hoods. We are here
to achieve clarity at all costs
about what's been demolished for us, even if that means
we must abandon what made us entitled to it.
Our losses have made us worthy of anything.

The question put here was:
Can the righteous man, though blameless, be enmeshed
in tribulations? He said. She said. One after another
gets up and forgets. The thread that winds through it all
is a portable image of the labyrinth.
It's easier to identify with the inhuman
when it comes to us in the form of leaves or fountains
and we, completely undeservedly, can believe we're participating
in a process of growth. And the man who bore the black spot

over his face also bore the time within him,
so he says, our time, and the digital beeping
that constantly recurs is the sign of this time,
puts small marks in it.

A new uncertainty has leaked into our faces
as luminous as the new globe on the horizon.
We walk on slabs of concrete surrounded by greenery.
The light lifts us, the light of public life,
for all we're worth.

(June 1989)

Evergreen

An array of the living is what most of us find
so annoying, the inability to love so many people
when they're gathered in a single place.
Even though each one has the theoretical possibility
of receiving your love, it is diluted to a slow foxtrot
worn smooth on the parquet.
That's when oxygen levels sink and the yawns arrive.
But someone opens a window, out of the others' sight
behind a drape or in an adjoining room
and the dance can continue in a coolness
saturated with sounds and smells from outside.
A head leans tenderly against a jacket shoulder, a hand
stands out against a naked back
narrowed to a V by a wine-red gown.
And several years later someone may suddenly start whistling
a melody that he shouldn't have anything to do with
in the back seat of a taxi. It was just that melody
that was being played when the change took place
and since then it has been, in spite of its banality,
so intimately connected with this that its sequence of notes
seems to signal the beginning of something new, though not
a single dance step has been changed or added.
That's how important the oxygen supply at an event can be!
Many believe that dance consists only of steps, unaware
that every great dancer carefully measures out small pauses
between the steps so the motion can send a surge
through both bodies, which the partner experiences as a feeling
generated by herself; it creates
a communion as between people drowning, so fragile
that any talk can disturb it.
For conversation has a tendency to emphasize
small disparities and finally make impossible

the type of communion that ballroom dancing evokes.
Quiet. Now they're playing again. It's the Good Night Waltz,
the evening's last chance for deeper contact.
Even before sunrise it will fall to the floor
like a wrinkled ballroom gown,
and this gives banality, too,
meaning and wordless melancholy.

Anamorphosis

Reflected in a convex mirror all faces acquire a harmonic form
while reality is grotesque and distorted,
raw material for perfect illusions.
This is called, I've learned, anamorphosis.
Now there are other questions that demand answers.

Where is the drunk conductor? He's the only one
who might explain the gaps between the black keys
on the piano. Why are there five of them and not six?
Is this something that strengthens the harmony or is it,
like the conductor's disappearance, something that causes mainly
confusion and gloom? *He has the key in his pocket.*
The piano key or the house key? It may not matter.
He's forgotten where he lives.

We trail him from bar to bar.
There are concerts underway everywhere but no one's conducting.
In late-night restaurants the orchestra members are sitting
and blowing into empty bottles.
And this sound suddenly becomes very important
because there was a risk that its hollowness
would remain unexpressed or be mistaken
for insignificance, emptiness.
That's how easy it is to forget that each instrument
has a hole as an important component, and this hole
is what gives the music its truth.
I don't say beauty because beauty is something
that wanders at will and only accidentally
unites itself with works of art.

The trail gradually gets clearer.
Fragments of him glint in shattered vodka glasses.

We gather them up, but some pieces are still missing.
Everything has its limits.
In painting they're defined by the frame.
Here in the improbable throng, by the disappointment that sets in
when you find the one you're searching for.

The Voyage

The need to laugh at the abyss can sometimes be deeper
than the abyss itself, late at night
at a checked tablecloth in the kitchen where rust spots from the grapes
carry over into your dreams together with all the people
the conversation was about. So many limbs
twisted around one another, yet never as in the Baroque paintings
where those in despair tumble toward the abyss,
but sooner with a grace so slow
that none of them really detect the fall,
since they think they're holding each other up. And naturally,
it isn't the precipice that's the threat
but the perpetual accumulation of trivialities,
which in the end make it not at all a matter of
"suns that some cruel angel whips around," not one huge
bleeding wound but multitudes of small irritating pimples.
Perhaps they're protection against the great wounds,
small practice questions in advance of the real problems.
They can be like insects, more irritating
on account of their number and persistence than by virtue of any
    "danger,"
a word all too often used as a synonym for The Great Maw
and not for the small mouths that perpetually eat us
the way printer's ink eats words. But the great ink spot ...
the great sore spot is a snake-charmer.
It gets the lines to dance on the brow of the precipice
as if that could mean something.

The Flute Player

What is important now is to be completely still,
to let you take the first step and drape me
in a loneliness that resembles a deeper communion.
Words like *secret* or *mystery*
have nothing to do with this. Everything about you
is visible but also, paradoxically, audible.
Your nakedness is so absolute that your soul
takes form as light and shadow playing over your body.

Your beauty would have been almost too consummate
if time hadn't put its mark on your body:
a crack across the calves, one heel missing
and the toes on the same foot crushed, a worn spot
on the knee and the fingers around the flute broken off.
The ear and nose too have acquired slight flaws.
And yet the angles and proportions are so perfect
that in histories of art there are pictures
where academics have tried with straight black lines
to elucidate your symmetry, make it universal
almost like a figure in geometry.

No matter what forms one inscribes you into,
you aren't there!
For one instant at the most, you passed through them.
The next moment wasn't given to us
when you stood up, put your flute aside
and took the first step out of your picture.
That moment you took with you, and all the following ones
a yellowed strip of film that has long since crumbled
into the invisibility that all past lives become.
To us there remains only the skeleton of a posed moment,
fossilized, and yet still vibrating with life from the others.

You do not meet my gaze
even though the eye that I can see is open.
It seems fixed on the note that hasn't yet left your flute.
But the melody can still be read in your face
and in your body, different for each person who listens
so it has an infinite number of possibilities,
is richer, yes truer,
if truth can be multiplied,
which I believe it can.
You play each one of us, and we
only our own imperfection.

Where does love enter in?
That is an important question, for it is apparent
that someone has chiseled his love into the stone
and this love is you.
It is offered across the ages to whoever
is capable of giving and receiving
a love as strong as marble.

Then, and only then, can the intensity of our own love
be what determines if it's requited.
Nothing else can free you from the permanence
where you are fettered
and let you take part in a life that resembles ours,
though we have learned to carry on with lower expectations
and persevere in an existence where the great passions
have been removed to other stages than the ones we tread.
Perhaps we are locked in our lives
as surely as you are in the stone.
In that case it's your love that is our freedom.
In that case our freedom is the stone.

Like Stars Half-quenched in Mists of Silver Dew

The smile does not exist in *the smile*.
It moves from word to word,
and from one person to another at the garden table
where they're shelling peas.
They don't even look up.
That's how important are these rosaries of green beads
running through their fingers.
They think of nothing else. And in the scenario
the letters near the margins have been lost in photocopying.
In theory this makes the lines infinite, as full of oxygen
as the air above the lake at the end of the garden.
Living characters stand there, transparent
as if made of water or glass.
When I come closer some of them vanish
while others take on sharper outlines.
Two of them are hoisting sails on a boat.
They've taken off their jackets and the wind carries them
through air and water in shirts whiter than the sails.
How did it go after that?
All that remains is the memory that it went on,
but no one remembers if this was the beginning of a tragedy
that ended with washed-up bodies covered by a sail
and women on a shore who recall the first
tentative words—"I knew you would come."
The word *velocity* also seems, in an indeterminable way,
to be associated with the scene. This is a paper play.
It was sold but never produced.
And yet there's still a mild breeze blowing.
We speak of "the wind's caress," the ultimate proof
that the earth moves and that this motion
is erotic and airy in clothes and curtains.
She's sitting at one end of the table.

The peas are rolling in all directions.
Her dress has a pattern of daisies.
If she made a sharp movement
petals would rain down over the table.
But she makes no sharp movements.

Two of Linnaeus's Apprentices Chasing
an Admiral Butterfly

To wake up under a butterfly wing that's falling apart.
Flashes from dull razor blades cut through, in step with the sound
that fades back to where we came from.
Time to get ready to move, hold up a shoe
for closer inspection. In this we will set out on our journey.
It already knows the feel of the earth against its skin,
has died once before, it became hide
laced around our hides, and the tongue
formulates dry words about dust and scattered visions,
castles and pennants stubbornly quivering so far away
that it doesn't matter if they exist or not
over there where we in any case only arrive
in order to dissolve

        as it happens,
and honey delicate in the air. Clouds of pollen
powder our wigs. Butterflies flutter above manure piles.
The sunset glowed inside them all night, pierced
by a dung-fork. Everything we touch gives the impression
of wanting to burst, days with overnight summer-ice.
We'll have to step more gingerly
so nothing will be startled by our tracks. A breath
can detonate the charge from within. How fragile everything is,
how taut the admiral's wing. How long
the journey is from what we've never had
to what we must lose
        when science's worldview
is cracked by radiant singularities. On distant continents
this wing will be our comforter once more
amid rich beds of herbs. That's roughly how the words go
in the lovely summer hymn we're chasing
under the greenwood tree.

Birdsong

"I was not born to die," but like the other small birds,
to keep twittering until the traffic drowns us out.
My consciousness is not a one-room nest, no—sooner
a swarm of sparrows—a little scattered
yet not without coherence.

What you know as my appearance I do not see myself.
Likewise with my voice. I don't hear it.
It comes out of me and often bewilders me.
What I know as me is everything that keeps fluttering around me
and only stops when you are here
and only you can see me now, and this silent room is you,
and this brief moment too is you, and this white breast
is you, and this soft thigh is you, and this deep hole
is you, and this consciousness,
and I am you

       and when you leave here
I am the sparrows twittering in your ear.

My Winterland

1.

It's the years I'm writing here
and what remains of them. It's the signs
and their arrival was expected. It's a laugh
that went missing. The stone on my chest will be moved,
but not today. The move will take place tomorrow.
It's a matter of seconds but how long are they?
It's from this house that winter comes,
run-down, quivering remnant, at hand.

Came from there with dignity intact,
sucking on a thread of my wool sweater. A headwind in my ears.
Soon it is gone. A child of many sorrows in a ridiculous hat
with a snap that makes a mark on the skin under his chin.
The winter street leaves us in the lurch, stretches into a field of view
where the sturdy bandy players are chasing something red and icy
that is winter's heart. The echoes from the lake.
They slap with their bandies but the power of the cold doesn't crack.
A can of frozen varnish under snow and tarpaulin, a hint
of sun-glitter and the play of waves

                           across the floor of the foyer.
There must be sunshine outside. It's so dark in the stairwell.
Piles of shoes that have stopped stumbling around.
The galoshes shelf. That's what it was called, and feet hurry by
in passing. Here there isn't a single thought
that can be compared to a room.
The hat shelf so high up that piles of headgear
are forgotten because no one can reach them.

My spot is here among the shoes, while the steps
continue up the stairs
to apartments so bright they're invisible.

It was to these white wards that my thoughts led me.
I thought, and what I thought was a wintry condition,
for others just a margin where the eye stops
only to go on reading one line further down.
It's continued that way. The furniture has white slipcovers.
We must be somewhere near the magnetic pole.
It was my job to calculate exactly where to plant the flag.
My only aids a school ruler, a broken pair of compasses,
a letter scale to weigh the winter light on.
It was all in the book I took home from the library
on my kick-sled, but the pages were so cold
they froze my fingertips.
The cold was still in my shoes far into May
and the fragrance of the arctic lilac.

2.

Was there a bumbling mercy,
knitted mittens in drawers, relatives trading stiff embraces
which one can only overcome by describing them?
In this way the stone can be moved, can leave a lane in the snow
like the runners of grass left rolled out when you build
snowmen. Charcoal eyes. Gravel for teeth,
indiscernible after the snow has melted.
Not even experts can distinguish water
that once was snow from ordinary water.
There's a draft from all corners of the cosmos,
which shrinks whenever the barometer's low, I crawl

on all fours, wearing out my pants,
damp rises, a musty winter.
The point of the compasses makes a hole in the exercise book.
Graph paper has always driven me crazy
and the circumference of the graphite circle just won't close.
The telescope finally makes the world round again.
Was there a fumbling forgiveness?

Everything was too bundled up, a red-nosed dread,
people at even distances from one another
like mailboxes. Every snowflake is a copy
of all the others. Don't believe anything else. The sled-runners
draw the borders between snow and snow, the spruces are bereft
of most of their glitter, flung onto the ground.
The badger's pulse in its winter den is down to one heartbeat a day
but that beat is heavy as a sledgehammer. Everything was the cold's fault,
but above the sofa there hung other landscapes.
Those were the ones I came from. The pictures of them have darkened
but in reality they would be radiant in arctic light.
If not for the stone.

    I'm writing this
and waxing my skis with tears. It's a day
when winter is all that happens. The plings from a music box
roam far and wide, a perpetual melody.
It begins where it ends. When we arrive there
we will see the icicles fall, not there but from a house
we've left, the floor gilded by varnish, rag carpets scrubbed
by the break-up of the ice when the water once again gushes out,
a sacred spring, but darker, the rumbling
from a thousand stones rolling away. The center is irrelevant
when everything is moving and it's tomorrow
where I am, without earflaps, without memories,
my scarf a flag wherever the wind is blowing.

from *The Main Stage*

1995

The Figure Skater

1.

What made me imagine I could fly?
It was a mistake, but a mistake
that gave me much delight,
broadened prospects, conversations with winged friends.
But I myself was the vortex,
I spin myself into
my sweater's wool,
centrifuge
the visible into spirit,
watch out
for black water.
Who could have believed
it would be possible
to escape for so long
the meanings of obliteration?

There is no limit
to how many faces you can have
rotating
around an imaginary axis,
alone and at the same time multiplied,
without succumbing to
the urge to vanish in the air,
to become a vacuum,
and in that way evade
the criminal light
that deadens the brilliant luster
of toe-caps and coiffures.

Speed is the ultimate visibility
made invisible as motion
inscribed in
circles   circles
me out
writes me into
visibility
into motion.

Figure-frozen there.

2.

In outer appearance the idea is the carousel's:
to spin to music and become a flicker
of horses' heads and gilded boats,
a laugh that spins faster and faster
but suddenly in a slow glide transforms
from rotation into something that can't be interpreted
without violins, for only this instrument
has the elegance of an ice skate gliding on the ice,
as cold and shiny as steel and yet modulated
into something that recalls the flight of gliders
though here the wind blows from within.

In this way I've spun myself into the music
until the music and I are one and move
as if the melody were spandex on my body.
Together we are images of a future
since we are performing something that doesn't yet exist,
but don't even think about asking me for examples!
I prefer to speak of the wind that blows through us
and through the instruments, a tornado
that drops me in the sunshine beside some beachfront kiosk

where only the drawers full of dry ice bear witness
to who I am and where I come from.

How can these notes so meticulously mounted in tarnished silver
give me such an impression of limitlessness,
of being able to travel freely among seasons and places?
I don't understand it but I see
that it is so,
exactly as the melodies have said.

3.

How little we know about pain
when it's translated into motion! Yet we've all seen
how the skating princess frets when, panting in wet tights
she waits on tenterhooks for the numbers
that are the reward for all the gray mornings
with frozen bumps on the skating rink
and doggedly repeated elements of motion
that little by little are shaped into
a dizzying sequence of weightlessness.
Feel sorry for me!
So much frozen water around me,
so many faces piled on top of each other
in the hope that everything will end in a slip,
that the music will flow naked
through cold loudspeakers while I,
short-circuited, slide around on the ice,
my feet, carved air, sharp grooves

so close to the heart that another millimeter
would bring death, or at least the end of life.
But this narrow pass too leads out
to open plains of ice

where all outlines quickly merge in transformations,
impossible to convey except through transformations.
If happiness is what we strive for
then only the sea is large enough for this choreography.
Only the sea has plains commensurate
to those we carry within us,
but all too rarely does the sea freeze over.

So we are restricted to stadiums, where the architecture
limits our movements and closes the circle
until the point at its center is still
and recovers the contours
you think are mine.

The Palace of King Minos

The green grass makes a perfect conclusion
to this chess game. New prospects were constantly created
until everything erupted in a snore
that made the castle totter. The runners disappear among the olive trees.
Their jogging suits resemble the Lily Prince's clothes,
their pastel-colored diagonals through the landscape
are themselves the narrative. So tempting
to fill in all the missing details in Jugend style,
make the lilies into signs and the butterfly a hieroglyph
that flutters away undeciphered above the bull's horns.

The labyrinth is another matter. The labyrinth is internal
and the passageways leading up and out are countless.
The bees find them every day.
Boats pass by out there.
The whole cruise was prompted by an ennui
on which the waves now bestow a gently undulating significance,
crowned by fringes of foam from shore to sunset.

The black sails were hoisted by a careless error.
Everything turned out all right in the end, as everyone out there knows.
But here on the shore the sorrow emerges as so deep
that it will give its name for all time
to this sea, crystal clear
even in the eyes of the drowned.

Sketch (Skagen, Denmark)

Stitch a cloud, stitch apple blossoms, saunter in summer clothes
along the flat beach
that slopes down under the ocean's swelling crinolines.
Who hasn't grown up in a mental hospital?
Who isn't forever seeing road signs pointing back there?
The dining-room tables moved out into the garden
and the bottles arranged to block the death rays.
The idea was that everyone should be happy.
That's why complications had to come ashore
disguised as short composers
with slick mustaches and metronomic gaits,
promenading half-notes in black trousers.
A doll thrown into the corner of a sofa
by a child who's begun to grow up.
Shadows of leaves on their faces until the rain comes,
so thin it forms a film with fine sand on their glasses.
Forgetfulness arrives with the rain
and continues through the ground,
invisible, invisible but cool. Afterwards
is the moment that causes the most pain.
The beach is endless. Boats full of fish
turn back to the ocean. Gleam of phosphorus in the sand:
it's gull shit, powdery in your palm.
Taste it. That's what remains
of the sun.

The Golden Helmet

1.

Surely we still remember, some of us,
when we were called on to cast our vote
for imagination or reality.
There was someone—was it me?—who through the smoke
in the restaurant tried to discern a clarity
that included both imagination and mystery. But no,
putting two ballots in the envelope
was strictly forbidden. A laughing mouth
butted into the discussion, rattled off the names
of all the stations between Stockholm and Uppsala,
up and back in hexameters. There was a pause.
That's how easily we're disconcerted by meaningless knowledge,
and the compass needle that was to show us our heading
ends up pointing straight inside us.

And I can only remember Rosersberg just before the caesura,
that brief pause in the middle of the line, not unlike
the silence when the train stops at a station
and a crowd presses on with big bags,
preventing people from getting off. Likewise a poem
is packed almost against its will by unexpected guests
who put their feet on the seats, work on crosswords
and have loud conversations about this and that.
And yet perhaps they are our brothers,
as the man in the golden helmet
was at least Rembrandt's "presumed" brother.
His face is almost extinguished
but the gilded helmet shines through the centuries.

For a brother is still a brother,
even if he's sometimes placed
near the foot of the festal table
where swords are crossed and a solemn oath is sworn by all
to fight together. Did it occur to anyone then
that among the other swords extended
was one that no one was holding?
That sword belonged to freedom.
That was the only one behind which
two resolute eyes were not flashing.
How often knives and forks have been crossed
in commemoration of that moment
at banquets where everyone's sitting there in too-tight pants
and suddenly someone says "Whose freedom?"
And a sword that no one's holding
cuts right through the conversation.

2.

The voyage must constantly take us to the places
we know the least about, where we arrive in the wrong clothes
move awkwardly and speak hesitantly,
not knowing which language is spoken in the region.
Only there, we're sure, can we find ourselves.
Of course it's exciting
to go rolling through such unknown parts
but one day you nonetheless confront a choice
and many who've never voted for reality
meet it face to face
uncertain whether it comes from inside them.
There is a pause.

Then the train gets going again.
Outside the window we see a dazzlingly white landscape
but feel the winter air only as a draft
through the cigarette smoke. Nor does traveling
offer any real sense of freedom
as long as the train follows the rails and we're continually
meeting oncoming trains full of people
whose longing drives them to the places we're coming from.
And again the landscape stops
in the middle of a sentence.

We'd planned on climbing the mountain
but the clouds piled up
and the air is very thin on the summits.
We walked around, we ate our sandwiches
at the rest stops along the highway.
You always arrive somewhere or other,
but each time both the destination and the visitors
seem more and more talked out,
more and more like memories of themselves.
In a pocket we find a half-empty pack of gum
from some other year but with quite a lot of flavor left.
We chew our way through it
as if through ancient meters
in fact devised for heroism and feats of arms.

3.

What became of those who cast their votes for imagination?
And where are those now who cast theirs for reality?
Did they move out into their landscapes and disappear there?
No more phone calls.
Every one of them walks through thin rain to the polling place
and puts an autumn leaf in the envelope.

All the perplexity about who "I" am
is nothing compared to the great question: who "we" are.
No one dares to touch that.
It would take us far too deep into the Folk
that once gave rise to myths and fairy tales.
In time our love is filled
by so much else, grows richer
without becoming freer on that account. And the swords
that were supposed to blaze a trail for it
halt at a clear-cut. What's left to worship
when freedom wanders among ruins?
On the doors we read the names of people we once knew,
but our joy that the key still fits
changes to disappointment that no one lives there anymore.
Of what avail, o brother, the gleam of your golden helm?
The ocean we dreamt of has flooded us out
and the horizon is filled by lifeboats
with provisions that will last as long as the night.
And it took the whole of this night to realize
that what ripped through
all our watertight bulkheads
was only the tip of the iceberg.

How far from one another can we get
without vanishing completely? We rattle off the names
of stations that we've long since passed
and complain that the earth is different
from the other heavenly bodies
by dint of its flatness and because
it does not radiate any light.
And yet we gathered once around a glow
that came from it or from us.
What we call extinction
does not lie before us.
We carry it with us under the golden helmet.

Can we ever throw it off and gather
at the intersection of two parallel streets
in the restaurant The Golden Helmet
after closing time?

The Main Stage

It's snowing in the streetlamp's shining cone
and not only there, most likely the whole night
is filled with falling snow, a plaster mask
on a face that's been renewed by plastic surgery
but isn't ready yet to break out of its hard cocoon.
The healing takes place in the dark, and the dark
has a place in us where we find the courage
to endure the knife that carves beauty
into our faces. Afterwards we can return from there
to a new name and a new death
while the white powder runs
through our fingers, runs and runs
through our fingers.

If you left your room, went out
and came back fifteen minutes later,
your first footsteps would be erased by then.
Meanwhile new faces have already made
"an indelible impression" in the throng on the Main Stage
where what used to be gets lost in the deep pile of the plush.
If we've been here without leaving any tracks,
have we been here? Don't we all deserve
thundering applause before we stream out
of the enormous wedding-cake theater?
For a few minutes more we speak in blank verse.
After that, in gray overcoats, we play the night,
which is nothing but a darkened stage
where someone's forgotten to turn off a spotlight
though everyone's stepped out of the spot.

In the rows of seats the velvet has gone dark
along with programs left behind. Everything plays itself,
including the box seats, whose gilt
is only a myth about a vanished golden age
when the crystal chandeliers could light up the theater
and at the same time reflect it in their prisms,
multiplied into a thousand miniatures.
The stage is enclosed in each crystal.
There each night *The Tempest* plays.
Now it's blowing through the world.

We hear the crystals rattling.

The People Who Envisioned the Garden Cities

The people who envisioned the garden cities are gathered
under high, fair skies.
On the table there are sheets of paper where in pale blue lines
they've drawn up the outlines of their dreams.
The apple trees are still so small that they can't
sit under them, but their thoughts
move at the same height as the apple blossoms
and are pollinated amid the buzz of small bronze-colored bees
so they can bear fruit on the other side of summer.
"In a dimly seen future," someone says,
when women lean ladders against the trees
and hands dissolved into mist bend the branches aside.
A suitcase under the trees is filled with Sävstaholm and Hampus apples.
Swirling leaves make up the ground.
Under them, with blind fingers,
roots extract
water from mist.

For it is the future's thoughts that need to be thought,
as in pruning trees the point is to find branches
that can sprout and bear fruit,
then take a step back
and, with a cheerful "alley-oop!", fling your beret through the branches
to see if they're sparse enough.
For it's important that the sky be visible between the branches
and that there be room for sunbeams to get through.
In fact this is the basic idea:
to make room for the sun in our lives.

The people who envisioned the garden cities
walk over pine-covered hills in trench coats.
They light pipes, mumble, point here and there

among bloodshot granite and dark pines.
Someone said the word "daycare." Everyone nodded.
The sisters Lagerlund came up
as the right persons to take charge.
A beach at Solvik, said another,
where boys in a Mälar-30 can sail close to the floating booms
to peep into the ladies' half and then
tack away, red-faced and giggling.
Then the discussion turned to traffic, a streetcar line
between the back yards. They talked about the color of the cars.
Blue, someone said.
Isaac Grünewald's name was mentioned.
He should be the man
to mix the sky-blue color
that would complement the vermilion of the buses.
And if they built a white streetcar terminal at Alvik
in the current functional style, they would have
a symphony in the hues of the tricolor.
Someone said the word "liberty," someone else "equality."
In their minds the little streetcar
is already in motion
between Park Boulevard and Clover Road.

They talked about private houses, apartment blocks, balconies
and about small garden allotments for people of lesser means,
perhaps with room for just one tree, but together
they'd still make a sea of apple blossoms.
Birdhouses also came up, but they agreed
that at this stage it wasn't necessary
to get into planning at that level of detail.
Yet the thought made someone else
associate with hangars.
An airport was mentioned, for they all shared the view
that their idyllic spot must be linked not only
with the city on the other side of the bridge

but with the world.
The old windmill at Lillsjön could serve
as a suitable landmark for pilots who, after crossing the Atlantic,
were searching with tired eyes for the runway.
They all saw how symbolic it was that a building with wings
that had once milled grain for the peasants
would now guide aircraft back to the earth.
And they talked about rows of lights, because someone
realized that in the dusk you could see only the dusk
and in the darkness only darkness, and now the day was over.
Time to fold up the survey maps
and sum up: Now that we've envisioned a future,
others will have to give it substance with their lives.
Our job was to keep the city from suffocating,
to construct a barrier of fruit trees against death by soot.
But we can't build happiness itself,
only create the conditions for it.
That was the meaning of our dreams,
to arrive not at a conclusion but at a beginning,
to reach the period that starts a sentence.

The Academy of Music

With each day the bronze horses in the square
pull the building closer to the unknown.
Nights they sleep under horse-blankets made of snow.
Like the freemasons they know that secrets
lose their power when they're no longer kept secret.
And here I am in these luxurious surroundings,
deserted piano salons where Christina Nilsson hangs
framed in gold as Ophelia
and the music stands' skeletons line up and fall over.
All day yesterday I could hear the piano tuner's one-note strokes
on the keyboard. That sound of the last nails going in.
Today there's an audition. The music professors are walking around
pale with responsibility for the day's verdicts.
The music students are sitting there in their finest and massaging their
    fingers,
for there are cold drafts through these rooms.
And whoever fails will float to the surface this spring
in the water-lily pond. It would seem
that when a musician dies, flowers spring up
in the same color as the dress she was wearing
at the audition when her hands suddenly started trembling
and the keyboard spread out its skull-like grin.
So much ivory! So many dead people!
You can catch their scent
in the flower shops, heavy and damp, when the salesgirl
with her nails polished a dark red
binds twine around stalks and rustles tissue paper.
The crash when she's punched in the total and the register drawer
hurtles out is a reminder, a fortissimo chord
followed by a long silence that is the true music
all notes are trying to interpret, just as the flowers
that spring up from the earth with their happy colors

are trying to tell about the darkness down there.
I would very much like to believe them, I want to believe
everything related by fragrance and fantasy.

The Last Summer Holiday

These woods were so old
that at night you could hear cows puffing and blowing there.
These roads were so old
that on my endless rambles I was accompanied
by a small white cloud around my shoes
and a similar cloud high above my head.
A Volvo PV rolled out of the woods, full of villagers.
They had traveled many miles to find out
who I was and where I was heading.
I sat down on a milk-loading stand and lit my pipe.
I pointed at the white cloud up there.
They understood.
He's going to graduate next year.
I pointed at the tobacco pouch
with Count Hamilton in braided kepi.
They understood:
then the cavalry; but after that?
I stirred the clouds with my hand.
After that we know nothing.
They waved goodbye, started the car
and turned onto the side road that went to Smedjebacken.

It was only 1960
but the birches were already yellow.
At the youth hostel in Särnaheden
a young English geologist arrived
from the other direction, from up on the mountain.
His knapsack was filled with rocks
and a can of mushroom soup.
He displayed his blistered feet while he made his soup.
The next day he hobbled off, doubled up
with a whole mountain on his back.

And as for me, I was equally weighed down
by last year's summer love, which maybe,
just maybe had survived the winter. So fragile
are such loves that they fill books with flowers
that many years later turn up pressed in used book stores.
Thus a great deal of literature is an herbal
and can be parsed only by one who's learned the language of flowers.

I didn't even know the names
of half the flowers in the roadside ditch.
The bumblebees circled in wide arcs
around Leksand, where I was headed.
In Dan Andersson country poetic melancholy grew
so large that only the massif could fill it
and yet it remained weightless.
The wind was so despairing, despair blew
the washing from the line,
blew shirts, pants up into the trees
which under full sail heeled around in the storm
while the heather surged in wave after wave.
The lookout tower was so perforated by lovers' initials
that the clouds squeezed into it
and made it risky to climb up.
Receding ridges without end
drifted their blue mist into me.

The Dalälven River, a waterway opening inward,
black with silver flashes, gliding toward fluid blue.
The woods fell and fell down to the water
floated down toward the sawmill.
The final stroke of the bow.
I saw last summer's love and she saw me.
We realized we wouldn't survive yet another winter.
I maintained ongoing contact
with Hermod's correspondence school.

Bent over Latin grammar I read:
amo, amas, amat, amamus, amatis, amant
and so on in every tense. So much love!
I could have loved. You could have loved.
The same refrain was played every Wednesday night
on the dance floor at Hjortnäs pier
by a trio from Borlänge with accordion, guitar and bass.
It was the last dance. The very last.
The steamboat *Gustaf Wasa* had already blown its whistle three times.
That was the signal for the return trip.

The boat too was accompanied by its cloud
just as we are escorted by clouds.
They obscure what lies before us.
They obscure what lies behind us.
They rise overhead and blot out thousands of stars
while we travel back between shores
where the houses darken into the night
and settle in, where people darken
into the houses and settle down.
The moon's bright pillar is a wall of water.
You've already traveled so far in moonlight
that shimmer has become reality.
Of course there will be people in the future.
Under heavy wall-clocks they've been waiting
since the beginning of time
for you to get home.

Walk through Autumn's Beauty

Karin Harding 1902–1993

1.

Once again this vision: I see you coming
out of the dark building in your nurse's uniform,
a white butterfly under black foliage.
It's the place of your death looking for you
and you're not there, and you are there,
walk through autumn's beauty, completely transparent,
for winter is already whitening the lakes and rivers
and their breaths are mist in the cold air.
We speak of it so carefully, as if it
could break at any moment,
though nothing's frozen over yet.
And we have no other miracles to desire
than trees and butterflies, and this is no time for butterflies.
The leaves fall into the water, small vessels
that drift away from land. They're what remains
of your thoughts when they've been exposed to daylight for too long.
The network of veins is still fully distinguishable
but so brittle that a finger's touch
would turn it to powder.

It's no longer possible to write you back into the life
you've aged into and are now getting ready to leave.
In the dark building the empty elevators move
from floor to floor of hallways and silent wards,
blurry pictures from a consciousness that's slowly emptying.
These days most often grief arrives before death,
wearing whatever's available for the occasion.
It would seem it's almost always trees.
Grieving needs its trees.

We think it's from them that the rushing sound comes,
but it isn't from them, isn't from them.
They stand there waiting for you to come their way
but your musings can no longer invade their crowns.
The branches point onward, beyond something
that for simplicity's sake we can call "the tree line,"
but that doesn't automatically mark the boundary of our world.
Not automatically and not definitively, just as the end of the year
doesn't imply the end of time, only a dry little click
in our wristwatch when a new digit pops up on the face.
Absence of boundaries is our normal condition.
Everything else is mechanical time and misunderstood geography,
but through whatever seems ready to break at the next moment
there streams something we recognize from music.
When it is named it begins to disintegrate, when it's touched
the song falls silent

            and we are left behind, pathetic conductors
of an orchestra who've packed up their instruments,
glanced sidelong at their watches and gone out through a door
labeled EXIT in green letters. The signs
that just now seemed so meaningful lose their magic
and become haphazard semaphores in front of the empty ditch
where dirty water is bordered by scraggly grass.
The black-clad choir consists of jackdaws
whose numbers compensate for their lack of range
while the light advances across the field, obliterates the vision
in which you leave the hospital building
disguised as yourself as a young nurse

and behind you the walls crash together
because nothing built of stone
can endure so much light in motion,
passing through the world and burning it up.
That's why the fever always precedes the silence

when the rooms empty of their shadows, which now are us,
while you dress in light
and prepare yourself.

2.

I cycle from the hospital, between trees and grief, past the house trailers at
the Ängby Public Beach, and above the tree-tops I see the black smoke
from the burning tennis hall at Alvik, soon to be charcoal, with the ten-
nis players in whites wandering around the sooty ruins.
You die in me in the sunshine outside the Central Station, where the caril-
lon in the town hall's tower vibrates piercingly in the air.
You die in me on the train to Gothenburg, where a manic girl comes over
to me in the restaurant car and quotes Rilke: "to be no-one's sleep under
so many lids"
and then shouts: "There's a bunch of cows standing there shitting!" in pas-
tures where the birches have only a few yellow leaves amid the green
rushing of eyelids, which droop shut, droop shut over No-one's sleep.
And I return along three hundred miles of dozing leaves and you lie in
the bed and pull the long tube out of your nose and the nurse comes
running and moves it so the nutrients can trickle down into the white
washbasin.
As if you wanted to show that sleep is all, yes sleep is now all that your eyes
wish for.

3.

I sit on the chair by the bedside.
Just you and me in the room.
Almost imperceptibly,
just me in the room.

Estate Inventory

It's so cold in here
among the objects of our childhood.
The gas heating has been turned down, since no one lives here anymore
aside from a fatigue that comes from far away
and will have power over me forever.
These tables and chairs, plates and forks—
will they forget us, our suburban naiveté,
and bereft of history find their places
under new lamps, in other neighborhoods?
It was an exhibition almost no one attended
since we were the only ones called on to see the objects
that formed us and that bear impressions of who we were.
So much was made of crepe paper,
it rustles, gray-blue, rough, almost old-fashioned,
while the floor's silence grows
waiting
for the telephone to be hooked up again.

from *Parlor Music*

2001

Dante Gabriel Rossetti

D o you know the bit about the shadow? He
A lone was accompanied by his shadow and
N aturally that made him less real than the figures he talked to
T hrough the unwashed window of dream—
E ver-cloudy map of the life of the dead.

G linting brass, that's where
A ll music comes from, not from the clouds or the
B lue-on-blue above them. Must they decay and be
R ipped to shreds? So rarely do women ascend in radiance
I n this land of fog. Rare for
E ven the fog to rise. Beatrice is bent over.
L ow on her belly hang her withered breasts.

R ed, deep red, almost purple
O rnaments and a velvet rosette, faded with age and
S oiled, wrapped around a tangled
S kein of golden hair that flows away,
E xposing a naked throat. Silent conversations
T ake place here with the angels, but in vain.
T he fog thickens again, and it will stay.
I s that all there is? Nothing else at all?

Paradiso

In the garden they are
the first humans.

The bridge is here for its own sake,
built over a pond
it takes two minutes to walk around,
the same time it takes their thoughts
to circle the leaf of a water lily
and return.

Almost unnoticeable movements
of darkness in the water
that alter everything
and nothing at all.

His lips graze her ear.
We are in Paradiso now,
he says.
This is the start of the long journey
to the Inferno.

The Doppelgangers

When a couple strolls through a park
and encounters another couple
in all respects their doppelgangers
then it's a bad omen.

The two couples stop
and stare at one another.
There are no words to exchange.

Those who meet themselves in a park
have nowhere else to go
but where the others came from,
to the remains of a love already played out
in a chilly apartment
where the rent hasn't been paid in months.

There they will search with their hands
for the people they once were
and listen at night
to the mice gnawing on letters and tubes of paint

until the only thing left
is the loneliness before it all began.

The Perfect City

One Wednesday three flights up in February
she had made the bed with clean sheets,
drawn the curtains,
for the window did not face the sky
but another building.

There was a storm that passed through.
So much blood in motion
through their bodies.

She floats amid her cascading hair.
The city outside is empty,
perfect and empty.
At its center stands their house,
casting silence through the streets.

Darkness waits in wells
to be hauled up, hauled up
in silent buckets
but the coldness of marble cannot be quenched.

We are only at the beginning of the story.
One day blood will flow from the whiteness.

The Birth

You can scarcely speak of light anymore
but you can sing it,
accompanied by stringed instruments
of a type that nowadays
survives only in historical museums
but was once every angel's possession.

The magpie on the stable roof is astonished,
astonished and embarrassed.
Reduced to silence during music lessons
with the heavenly choir,
it is the stable's cleric.
To it all things are black and white.
Only its tail feathers can catch
the heavenly light.

What remains of their love
is this stillborn child, bloody on the sheets
with his hands placed so they reach out toward his mother.
But his Father has claimed him back
and his scream is an eternal silence.

Larded with Sweet Flowers

In the night where I am not with her
she's been immersed in the cold bathtub.
Her face expresses nothing.
Her face expresses a great sorrow.

But she continues to sing,
weighed down by soggy flowers
she continues to sink
through the night where I am not.

Sheet after sheet of paper is burning.
Her letters were written to the flames.

To become a part of everything
she must first become nothing at all
and the song she sang
be plowed under with the potato haulm.

In the night where she is not
I bury my book.

In the Kingdom of Death

Every night she came back to him.
Life in the underworld was so sad.
She escorted him through the cities of the dead.
The people there were dressed in splendid costumes
and greeted him as if he were already one of them.
He slept late into the afternoon,
when he awakened with tears in his beard.
He ate his breakfast at the dinner hour.
Only at dusk did he venture into the streets.
The people there were more like shades
than those he met in the cities of the dead.
And again she walked by his side.
He asked: Who is tormented here?
She answered: Those who did not love each other enough.
He asked: Is that a sin?
She answered: It is grounds for eternal affliction.

Another night, another question:
And those who loved each other too much?
He saw a desolate city with empty streets.

Pre-Raphaelite Dance

It's in our sleep we dance so well
through fields of towering cowslip.
It's in the era before Raphael

before perspective came to light.
Darting through the air: a swallow.
It's in our sleep we dance so well.

Each person and each human act
take on the form they have inside us.
It's in the era before Raphael.

From yellow bells a melody rings,
the only song I wish to dance to.
It's in our sleep we dance so well.

A second-shard I see myself
as tiny, in the bird-eye's mirror.
It's in the era before Raphael.

Deep underground great maggots thunder
but the cowslips drown them out.
It's in our sleep we dance so well.
It's in the era before Raphael.

The Menagerie

Ideas arrived infrequently. When they came
he therefore tried to make as much of them
as possible, embellish and color them,
embroider them. When the menagerie idea arose
he filled the whole house with exotic creatures:
birds with plumage he didn't hesitate
to describe as Byzantine; these snagged his thoughts,
repeated them ad nauseam with crooked beaks
and fanatically blinking eyes, while the monkeys stuffed fleas in their
    mouths
and imitated the delicate colors of his palette
by displaying their purple rumps, even to visiting clergy.
The frustrated elephant never learned to wash the windows.
Wrinkled and gloomy, it stood there in the courtyard
in a big puddle, drinking the soapy water.
Like the ideas, the animals languished
in the raw, damp climate, dreaming of
more colorful landscapes, more passionate eras.
In the midst of this mess sat Dante Gabriel,
conversing with an angel. His sister
said her prayers: "Grant that he retain
the light of his eyes, his forceful intellect!"
But the fog had already enveloped him.
In this way the days passed
while the animals started chewing on one another
until all that remained of his original idea
was tragic fragments of bone and feather
that the charwoman carried out on her dustpan.

Imperfect Tense

The imperfect gnaws at us,
so much richer than the present,
and with women so beautiful
that the cat mews on the gravel walk.

It hears the sound of a thousand rodents
transforming the garden
into the past, the imperfect.

Yet a sea of flowers
still covers the black soil
just as his embroidered vest
covers the darkness in his heart.

Each flower has shown itself worthy
of having a portrait of its own.
Therefore he stands weeping in the garden.
His brush goes too slow.

The flowers wilt, the paint dries out.
The wardrobe stands there,
dark with her gowns:
they too are lifeless.

This is called "The Post-Romantic."
He calls it his life.

The Window Open to the River

How did his world sound? The rattle of a window latch;
a floorboard, rain long gone, the comb
through her hair. Golden, he says,
in the world he writes it is golden
and his hand glides over her back, more naked than the river,
quieter than the traffic over the bridges. Was there room
for anything else, undescribed? There was a great deal
whose job was to muffle impressions, spread shadows
when the gleam of the highlights became unbearable.
One can clearly make out a snuffling
coming from a heavy body, drunk or unhappy,
slightly groggy from interrupted sleep
or everything else—but only
if the listener feels at home in the gloom
where each shading is merely
a failed attempt to fend off a uniform gray.

A vest stretched over a huge belly,
its roundness set off by a watch chain—
this too can be a "hill of poetry." Pacing
back and forth in rooms more dismal than their own easy chairs
doesn't have to be meaningless just because
it's so obviously hopeless. The right to interpret
belongs to those who come later. They will give their meanings
to this murmuring in deserted hallways. But can they even decipher
the sound of a glass toppled over
and something viscous running out. Liqueur?
Can they be entrusted with the jumble
it took a lifetime to dream into being,
they who always get to have the last word,
and which word is that, yes
which word is that?

Now it's someone else's day and you enter it,
a day so close that the two of you grow through each other
and vanish through still lingering cities.
Voices approach one another, reproach one another,
grow more and more distant
in days that are mercilessly dated. The breathing,
yes the breathing too, that curio!
Its heaviness a lighter and lighter burden,
a dying never in the present, never near,
a shiver from far off, and through her hair a comb
from another era!

Museum

Touching the objects is of course forbidden,
but just getting too close can set off the alarm
and make a sleepy guard look up, annoyed, from his chair.
Between us and the pictures
there's a zone we mustn't step into.
That's how it has to be and the rule is reciprocal.
The object mustn't reveal itself either
by a sudden movement, an outstretched hand.
We are in a museum, a mouseion, the temple of the muses,
but no one sings here.
Is this "The House of Life"
surrounded by fog, black hedges, a wrought-iron fence
with sharp lance-tips along the top?

We walk through the galleries quickly
so the anguish won't cling to our clothes.
In time, artworks too are institutionalized
sit up in their beds like chronic patients
ashamed that the faint sprituality they exude
is scaring the visitors and making their speech hesitant and stilted.
Or do these rooms remind us more of a morgue
where visitors hope at all costs to avoid recognitions?
The debate between the dead and the not-yet-dead is about
whether beauty is a sign that content is missing.
About beauty the living have little to say.
They are the ones who speak of absence as something present.
The dead think about their long hair, how they haven't
combed it in the longest time.

People glance furtively at the brass plate that says
Dante Gabriel Rossetti (1821–1882). "He must be the one
whose wife killed herself. The one who put his poems in her coffin

'so they would be hers forever' and then,
when he needed them, had her grave dug up
so he could get them back. And I think their child
was as stillborn as these paintings." Then they look around,
spooked, and hurry on, as if they'd caught a glimpse
of her golden hair in the depths of the grave.

It's that easy to conclude the colors conceal
only decay. That easy for the longing and the pain
soon to grow a trifle laughable and mummified.
The same thing happens to those who've been close to us.
Imperceptibly the days throw open their doors faster and faster.
We go in and out through them and in time become
more and more old-fashioned. Anyone hooked on tales of adventure
who one day strikes out to hear the roosters crow
in the next village and the next, until they crow in a language
even roosters can't understand, sooner or later will find
in the sale bin of an antiquarian bookshop,
under the light of exhausted lamps,
the thoughts that made him set off in the first place.

The first mistake Dante Gabriel made
was doubtless to choose the prefix *pre-*. It pointed backward
like a road sign to motifs long since painted dry.
Yet he found there a well from which he and his friends
could haul up lapis lazuli and splatter it on one another
amid peals of delight. And there they found wine bottles
to uncork and songs it was still possible to sing.
There too a melancholy that lent their joy meaning
and clear colors and outlines. But everyone knows
that such spells are as fleeting as the starlings
that make a tree sing but, scattering
"to the four winds," leave only mute foliage behind,
for few are those who can capture birdsong with a brush.

"His sister wrote lovely poems," many say,
so different from the casual life he led.
Certainly true, but one who moves
in worldly circles—which are hardly concentric—
can snap up an impression amid the excitement, indeed a truth,
even while amusing himself, as when you open your pocket watch
and the gleam flashed by the case plays over the cheek
of a beautiful woman who catches it with a smile.
Yes, often a smile was the start of what later became
a poem or a "personal tragedy."

Did he already see at their first meeting
the sorrow that was to be theirs
precisely because he was so conversant with Renaissance smiles?
Who can answer questions like this one
and the others that jostle behind them?
Is it possible to imagine a comedy with a tragic ending,
a Beatrice whose clothes smell of bacon
from the smoky kitchen? Did it rain all the time?
Did he paint year after year in a light
that didn't exist, at least not there?
Could he measure up as an artist to what he observed?
Wasn't it more than the flowers, wasn't it also the women
he portrayed that became immortelles, eternal
but at the same time dry and without fragrance?
Was everything his fault, his insomnia self-inflicted,
and was his pain therefore less authentic?

Easier to answer the questions posed by death.
They are their own answers, a sheaf of buried poems
raised up into the light on shovels only to rot
as the secrets of the grave do "before the eyes of mortals."
He stood there caught in a pathetic pose,
a man in a Spanish cape whose vanity was greater than his grief
or at least appeared to be.

How could a human comedy like this one
end up with atonement drenched in light?
No, the sequel must proceed toward collapse and pathos,
and thus the patterns of the past were little help.
Through the wallpaper in the House of Life
came patches of damp and decay.
He hung his pictures over them.

Behind it all the thundering word
was of course Resurrection,
so powerful he had to keep it draped
in veils of color, unable as he was
to weave draperies of theology or philosophy.
Yes, even his flimsy cravats and perpetual Spanish capes
were pathetic mundane imitations of these curtains
designed to conceal something so tremendous
that cliffs split apart and even the angels scattered
like flocks of birds at a rifle shot.
What would be resurrected behind these clouds of feathers,
the body or the soul, his life force or hers?
He didn't know, knew only that he had to
keep working toward something that would hold,
but what something, and would it hold—or molder? Even that
he wasn't sure of.

All this made his eyes tired.
Yet he retained his ability to see goddesses
where others saw only milliners and barmaids.
Then he found his Persephone, married to his best friend,
who, against his will, we can suppose,
got to play the part of Pluto and design death's abode
and cut the alphabet that was to describe it
for a curious public. Yes, everything that surrounded
her and Dante Gabriel's love was designed by her husband
with a delicacy no one had believed he possessed.

A pansy in a vase on the table was her signal
that her husband had gone off to his weaving course or had left
for Arctic regions warmed only by the sled dogs' breath.
What is a spouse's role in a Romantic age
other than to suffer betrayal and tramp the frozen deck of a ship,
fleeing from one desolation to another?

Inevitably Dante Gabriel's love grew shabbier and shabbier,
soiled by treachery to the living and the dead, embedded
in a flatness discernible even now amid the matte colors
on the gift shops' birthday cards. Surely, fogged in
by mythology in the twilight, he must still have heard
the cry "You rogue!" like a trumpet blast
from the stone angel on the balustrade, a dissonant chord
among the shapes of the asters. When the spouse returned
he radiated the icy cold that many women
find so irresistible. Only then
did the thought of the children strike them.
What would happen to the children
and what did *they* think about all this?

Such a thought, once it had appeared,
excluded Dante Gabriel. To call him "forsaken"
would be to go too far, but many blossoms closed for him.
The flowers hid their faces when he walked by
and took on lilac-brown hues, which suggested
they preferred to seek out death in their own hearts
rather than follow him on his unsteady path
toward an ever more conspicuous carnality.
He mixed light red and vermilion,
strontium yellow, Indian yellow and Davy's Foundation White—
with laudanum, whiskey and melancholia. Was this
the formula that could rekindle
the warmth of a woman's skin, revive
the scent of canceled rendezvous?

Someone's gotten too close to the pictures. An unintended movement
has set the alarm bells ringing. After a period
of clarity and confusion the smog settles in again. Nothing
is any clearer than the smog anymore. Over the voices it rolls
a sleeplessness as blurry as the one Dante Gabriel
more and more often confounded with his Self, a mist whose outlines
he made his own. It was his cape,
his cravat. Ever more deeply enshrouded
he drifts in a thickening colorlessness
hoping to save yet another coil of hair
from No-more, Too-late, No-more.

The House Where the People in This Story Were Still Living

Plump green on creepers winding through the rain
that rinses the house till it gleams
and gathers in drops on the windows—shining eyes.
They observe figures walking under the branches
and raking leaves.

Their outlines can already be found
as patterns on tapestries and wallpaper
in drawing rooms, in drawing rooms
where silent betrayals under the chandeliers
make the roses molder away, the leaves fall
like the rain through the dark rooms.

Outside, grayness returns with the rooks,
the grayness returns to the fields
and the walls chew on the ivy with gray teeth.

The woman marvels to see that the sunbeams
do not pass through her body, not yet,
though vapor rises from the birdbaths
and the heat evaporates from her skin
to be cooled and become water again.

He makes love with her in the dark house,
until her body becomes a riverbed in the darkness.
Her husband sees everything.
He does not weep,
but he slowly dies

while the river carries off more and more,
out through the dark hallways,
down the steep stairs
to what used to be a garden.

The Garden of Proserpine

Nowhere,
nowhere in the heavens or on earth
did he find darkness
so sparkling with constellations
as in this room,
enveloped in her black, black hair.
Her bite from the pomegranate makes a wound
with the same shape as her mouth.
One day,
one day he will paint the sky
on the inside of a coffin lid.

The moths eat their way indiscriminately
through the wardrobes of the living
and the dead.
The only sound
is the murmur of pleated velvet
falling apart.

What seems to be a garden
is only a tapestry
where the plants are carnivorous.
Gracefully they dip down
and bite through one another's throats.

They lean in over our lives
uncomfortably close
to her throat and long arms,
whiter than the bathtub's enamel,
until what we called life is death
and death is our life.

The Daydream

Blind spots, there are blind spots of sun
here amidst the shadow-play of leaves, the only words
those of the language of flowers.
In the afternoon heat
in a completely unnatural way
she has climbed into the tree
where her thoughts
become the thoughts the tree is thinking.

Of course it's the blackness in the blackbird's song
that makes the tree burst out in green,
in leaves that have been cut
from her velvet dresses.
Their rooted dance
never ends, never ends,
not until the thoughts
have infected their veins
and shriveled them to paper,
rustling sketches
of what they once were.

From marshy ground the cattail will grow, the cataract
will fall when the sky splits inside the eye.
Whatever's blue can never be dissipated.
Everything else is in motion. All this
fed the earth, fed the tree, fled
into the burning wind.

The scent of honeysuckle,
only the scent of honeysuckle
proves this is true.

The House of Life

Houses too can die of grief, brick by brick,
even though "their time" hasn't come yet.
This doesn't mean that social life must cease in them
but the conversation loses some of its élan
just as the furniture loses its luster.
No one dares to say: "We're now in a house
that's about to die." No one uses the word *grief.*
Someone gets a bottle of furniture polish
and rubs and rubs but the face
that appears in the tabletop is the face
of a person living in a house that's started to die.
He's living there temporarily, perhaps light-heartedly,
but nonetheless amid grief as massive as a house.

"Leave me here," he cries,
or "Don't leave me here."
It doesn't much matter which. No one's listening.
Is it honey that's making his fingers stick together
and smearing the sleeves of this velvet suit? Who knows,
maybe the bees were also part of the house's grief, the honey
their clumsy attempt to console, the sugar water
their only reward. That's how killer bees arise, so heavily armored
that they can see nothing, hear nothing.
The future belongs to them. They will leave behind
centuries of blackened petals, severed pistils.

He hears so much. He sees so much.
Angels burn through the nights
but without casting light on the question: "Can something die
that has no heart?" Defeated wingbeats rattle away
over the ridgepoles. Was he the only one who saw the peacock
spread its tailfeather canopy

and be expunged by its own bloodcurdling shriek?
Who was prepared for this? Will even the starry sky be prepared
when its vault collapses onto him
and all the others who let themselves be guided
by miscast horoscopes to the night's derelict house?
Will there be time then to hurl oneself out
through the window whose glass
is adorned with motifs from the tales of King Arthur?
Cascades of colored shards, sharp as razors,
are what he sees.

"You should have let me go on sleeping
behind the dying walls," he says, "in the hope
that one day I might signify
something that was me."
In the Tristan Room she makes the bed for him.
"I can't lie to you," she says
but this statement too is a lie, the last one
before she follows the spiral banister up into the clouds.
He lies down on the cold sheet, alongside himself.
For safety's sake he lays a sword between them.

A Day That Wasn't His

So hard to imagine him outdoors
or rather "in the open air," in an openness
big as a cricket pitch and surrounded by elms.
If a flag is fluttering it's red-white-blue, yet not
a tricolor. He can't recall which color
stood for Fraternity—*that* he has experienced,
but maybe it's gone now. There's a river there
and a train that runs along the river. Doesn't it roll forward
mainly so it can pump out its little puffs of smoke against the sky
which otherwise would have been almost rudely free of clouds?
The faces glimpsed in the windows are pale,
like the faces of miners trapped in their shaft.
In any case they don't belong to living people—
that's an epithet we reserve for ourselves.

How many days where he didn't belong!
They remain unpainted because their motifs weren't his,
or not considered his, and those who could have claimed them weren't
    there.
So their copses and towns have no visitors, nor the inn
where an old music-hall singer is waiting almost desperately
for someone who remembers her to come by.
But no one comes by and no one remembers.
A great deal of food gets thrown out—lamb stew, fried potatoes,
everything the innkeeper and his family can't manage
to eat up themselves. Every passing train traveler knows this!
In the root cellar there's a swallow that's locked in. No one hears it.
That's how silent its panic is. Also his, which the poem is about
but which doesn't belong in it.
Yet here he is, walking around.
The dark coat is his.

Rossetti Sleepless in the Park

1

No, I'm not dead.
You left me here on the street corner at the end of a century
with my face turned toward the moonlight. It took so many years
for the veils of cloud to part, so many years that the books
I carried in my pocket and used to read in the park
began to fall apart.
That was in the days when angels
still came out in the dusk
to light streetlamps shaped into cast-iron flowers.
They pulled the light from the dark ground
and they too
had faces blotted out by moonlight.

Of course you can love everyone,
but when you've loved everyone
there's no one left,
only the rustle of clothing
rushing down with a sparkle
toward the end of a century—the last one,
soon to be the one before the last, or the next one.
So much had to be left behind,
unsaid.

I never painted myself
behind the white waterfall, standing erect.
There was so much in the way—
that's what I saw in the light of the streetlamps.
I saw how, in growing,
each tree took its life, as slowly as I was doing.
I dozed off and saw more clearly still

how the moonlight pulled leaf after leaf
off to its death. But this,
even this I could not learn to describe
before the smell of rotting pages put me to sleep.

2

Go on without me! I'll stay here under the tree
in this landscape by Piero della Frencesca
where I tend the horses while my queen
kneels before a foreign king
and offers precious gifts
in exchange for knowledge and peace.
That peace can be sensed here in the silence
that makes the gowns of the ladies in waiting fall in pleats
and flow outward in waves of silk
among the hills that seem to be Tuscany.
That's where I'd like to stay, enclosed
in a century that lasts a thousand years.

It's so long ago
she became my queen.
She held her cloak above me.
I knelt down with my gaze turned
upward toward the sky of cloth
that screened a second sky
covered in gold leaf.
Thát I was not destined to see—
not until now,
now that her cloak has been rent
by the weight of our grief.

The white horse turns its silky loins toward me
while the black one neighs coarsely in the face of my devotion.

Alongside them I wait,
empty of thoughts, but aware
that they're somewhere nearby,
ready to turn up wearing fresh colors.
The same old thoughts
completely new, as in poetry.

3

A few blocks further into insomnia
I catch a glimpse of the park.
"Gold and silver finely wrought, carmine and white lead."
Was I the one who wrote that canto?
How did it go from there?
"New emerald when it's freshly cut."
But even finer than these lines: the trees here,
angels that have folded their green wings
and dozed off standing up, to be reborn in the breeze.

Why strive for purity?
Once I had nothing if not that
but now my clothes are covered with spots of paint
among which I've been lost
in the new disintegration, the new exasperation
of dried-up watercourses, dried-off tears
at the impossibility of living outside the war
in the heart of a growing empire
and all the while adorning its surface
with screens of gardenias.
I'm not the only one who loves the surface.
This means that when my own surface crazes
I am no longer loved.

Something else is consuming the pictures
with an unsurpassed rapacity, and at a rate
my rebirth cannot match, a disgusting gullet
through which beauty has gone pouring down
into the growing empire of a gaping abdominal cavity
where even the daintiest pastries are transformed into …
You said it yourself; I couldn't write it.

Look in my face; my name is Might-have-been;
I am also called No-more, Too-late, Farewell.
I am no longer born anew.
I came here along streets so sad
that I couldn't walk them sober.
It's closing time
and the green angels are park attendants
for all this other greenery.

Gold brocade, give me gold brocade
so I can drape the naked truth:
a fat, groaning fellow who's carried out of the park
with the navel of his sweaty belly gazing
straight up toward a flaking pale blue sky,

and this man is me.

from *The Burning Child*

2003

Moment in Tibble

On the other side of the road
and beyond the sodden woodpile
the black horse is
jogging around in the drizzle,
gets a shock from the electrified fence,
starts galloping and kicking.
Across the pasture,
past the break of birches,
on the other side of the river
a freight train goes by.
The sound reaches
all the way over here.
Back there stands the mountain.
It can't be seen for the rainclouds,
but it's there.

There is a consciousness greater than humans',
that much we agree on, the horse and I.
Why else would we feel driven day after day
to investigate everything around us?

There is knowledge stored in the invisible mountain
and, on a lesser scale, in the wet rocks I dig up.
The knowledge dries out in the air.
So far I haven't learned
to interpret the rocks' language
or that of the roots,
which I chop out
because their trees aren't here anymore
to tell their stories.

A village shoemaker lived here before, people say,
and every Saturday treated the village boys to hooch.
The ground is full of discarded lasts
and shoe-soles marked by holes where the tacks rusted away.
If you hold them up against the sky
a row of bright dots runs around the edges.
I am the village's Heinrich Schliemann.
With my spade I discover that the story is true.
There are bottles here, smashed bottles.
They glitter like a Trojan helmet in the gravel.

It clears up. In the twilight
it clears up. A boy from the village
passes by on a mountain bike.
He stops on the road between me and the horse.
"There's a fantastic sunset tonight," he calls.
"You can get a great view from the crest of the hill over there!"
He knows about our project
and wants to help us out.
He's right.
Pink wads of cloud against a sky still light-blue
are thoughts worth exploring
high above our heads.

Lost?
I'm no more lost than the bumblebee among the wet lilacs.
A bit distracted, perhaps.
Things get clearer later at night
when I hear the shoemaker hammering.
No, it's the horse stamping in the stable
on the other side of the road.
The flies that he's brushed away with his tail
because they were disturbing his contemplation
are flitting around my face.
My thoughts move in a similarly

whimsical way. They're still buzzing around in the air,
still strolling around the tip of my nose,
then they rest a bit, in reflection
or at least in silence.
I swat myself
in self-defense.

The Wandering Shoemaker

Where did the shoemaker go?
He isn't dead. Shoemakers don't die,
they go out wandering. He left the house
for the seasons to pass through freely.
Having devoted his life to making shoes
he will now devote Eternity to wearing them out,
till all he made has been unmade
and Oblivion has taken over—and the saplings
that I spend my days chopping down.

Certainly in the background there was a curse
barren and wind-beaten as a gallows-hill.
But who remembers the Beginning now?
Have even curses managed to remain demonic?
We can only establish
that shoemakers are doomed to disappear.
The house remains and gazes down at the bend in the road
where he turned around one last time
and raised his hand in a silent farewell.
But I know that shoemakers never come back
—for then what meaning
would Eternity have, or wandering,
if the goal were to return?

That's what the black horse is brooding about.
He's standing on the other side of the road.
His long, wise teeth are chewing grass
that is forever renewed, forever renewed
from within the earth.

Watercolors

The mountain has returned. Precisely that blue color
it has today is the one I've long been waiting for.
A tortoise-shell butterfly flies right into my forehead
as I cycle down to the river on the winding road
with a strip of grass down the middle.
For a moment I think only butterfly thoughts,
slightly giddy ones that flutter off across the edge of the field.
Naked, I step into the river
where the reflection of the landscape
gleams in clearer colors than the landscape itself,
for one moment, one moment
before the wind passes over the surface.

My desire to write worse and worse poems
still isn't as strong as my yearning
to paint a really lousy watercolor
where a completely hopeless blue runs out into the water,
only distantly related to that blue
that just now seemed as momentous
as becoming water oneself and reflecting a mountain.

What luck I had on that June day in 1955!
The west wind and the daisies had arranged to meet
just where I had stretched out in the meadow.
Like our sisters the birches
we feel now and then the light breeze
of the earth's dizzying passage through space.
This was such a day.

So in fact we pass our whole lives in the heavens!
Not even if Professor Hedenius from Uppsala
had come by on a moped could he

have persuaded me to the contrary. Not on that day.
And yet I had no arguments,
only a box of watercolors, a bristly brush
and a soda bottle filled with water.
But I didn't paint that day. Not that day
and not today.
Just listening to the wind-rush
from our voyage through the heavens.

And this happened only a few kilometers off the main road
where a heavy timber truck is now hauling its rough logs,
the truck too on its way through the heavens.
For forty-two years I've been on my way back to this moment
when my spirit was clothed in grass and clouds.

Can anything grow from its own reflection?
I step out of the water,
as clean and cool as the birch my bike is propped against.
Even chopped up and stacked in woodpiles
the birch trunks preserve their clarity
as they wait for us to come back in winter
and start a fire in the wood stove with a newspaper from last summer
whose pages are yellowed by sunlight.
And we will look out through the window and say:
If there is a God
who still takes pleasure when incense is offered,
then nothing can appeal to him more
beneath the starry sky of winter nights
than the thin smoky fragrance of a birch
that in summer saw its image in a river.

Night in Tibble

First come the headlight beams,
igniting spruce trees, birch trunks, a red gable.
Then comes the engine sound, until everything goes dark again
and the trees fall silent into ebony.
Soon I won't know whether I'm growing hard of hearing
or the grasshoppers have died out,
taken their small violin cases made of grass and gone away
like the mammoths that one evening long ago
walked into the twilight and turned into haystacks.
Straight through the forest, just twenty meters from here
a piercing death-cry shrills from a creature
being carried off, most likely in the teeth of a fox.
I don't even know if it's a cat or a bird.
I know so little about animals, but death
I can recognize now.

Soon I hear other silences, new steps
from inside the ebony forest. A roe? A badger?
My imagination's so vivid, annoyingly vivid.
Someone's roving around in it trying to build a piano.
He's searching for the mammoths' legendary burial ground
in the middle of the forest, if the forest has a middle, or if even
the legend has a center filled with ivory.
He's not going to succeed. He will never
succeed, that diligent piano-builder.
In the end he'll wind up with something absurd,
a piano with only black keys
in a forest where the trees have darkened,
every last one of them,
the birches as well, fifty-two birches,
exactly as many as the missing keys.

Poem That Starts with a Line from Fats Waller

Blue turning gray over you
as you wield a duller and duller pair of shears
to prune the lilacs outside the kitchen window
so your thoughts can reach further. Surely it's the case
that each leaf you tear off the wall calendar
is flimsy paper between you and no further. Just as surely,
just as surely certain intervals yield a blue insight
that your visual field is growing every day, words approaching
tentative conversations under ever wider skies.
Far into the dusk, roofs preserve the light for those
whom piano improvs on the radio make attentive
to its slow extinction on the roofing tiles
in a village adrift through darkening fields of rye.

Is it possible to think without mountains nearby?
They still delight in being gazed on
as they stretch out between you and infinity
enveloped in thoughts that only they can stop from vanishing
into the place where everything you thought you knew
lacks words. There is such a thing
as a peaceful unease, an alert slumber,
a thought so slow that if it set out for a star
it would be extinguished before it arrived.

The thought or the star? What does it matter?
What difference does a vague reference make
in the face of extinction? But everything that reaches the mountain
comes back, comes back
unextinguished, comes back
blue.

Embers

Nothing is colder than a cast-iron stove
the night has blown out.
Not the constellations. Not the raindrops in the spruce trees.
The metal aches back
to the icy glow inside the mountain,
the mountain that comes closer every day.

Everything submits to the wind, succumbs
to the wind, in which it's all whipped
across stretches of forest, acres of fields.
The apples start glowing.
We planted the Red Astrakhans through slushy snow one spring day
when the wagtails ruffled themselves into balls
and drew close to the house to be warmed by its wood.
So wearying to glow.
The apples soon give up.
But it isn't gravity
that makes them let go,
rather the longing of the fruit
for the wet grass.

How to distinguish between flying
and falling? Between glowing
and going out?
Don't ask the crow.
It flaps ash-gray, soot-black
as an iron stove
from September to October.

Return Visit, October

The black horse isn't here anymore.
I feel his absence even as it makes
the landscape's sounds and movements more prominent.
There is so much sky here
that before I've managed to describe a section of it
all the other ones have been transformed and shifted around,
for the movements of clouds and language
can never be identical
and Eternity can not be captured in snippets.

So much better, then, to concentrate on
what's missing from the blue fields
among the smoke-colored clouds with light breaking through
—humans are missing there, and horses.
Only in legend do they sail above the treetops,
sail upward as rejoicing music
rises from the hills, yes from the very hills.

And here I can almost hear it
as I cycle through the sound of rain-slick leaves.
This must be how the dead perceive it
—a weightless gliding past the birches
which whoosh with great dignity lest they be mistaken
for the flighty aspens. That yellow speckling
is their way of saying goodbye. The October light
encompasses me as I encompass
the wet country road in myself
on the blue bike.

"If we could be content with a world
that was only like a fleeting dream,
could we settle for the world as an idea,

like the final and ultimate one, in which our minds find peace?"
No, I can never find peace unless I know
whether the wind that blows on the trees
until their colors begin to glow
is the same breath
that blows through me.

In the October darkness many years from now
you will see a bicycle lamp, jumpily journeying
like the shoemaker through eternity,
and you will not know
if that lamp is mine, or even
if I'm living or I've died.

Triptych for Nils Kölare

The Garden

All that's needed
is a bridge with seven arches,
which, reflected in the river, become seven circles
unfathomably filled with olive green,
exactly the color the cows love
to drink in the twilight
before jogging off with wet muzzles
beneath the shadows of leafy trees
in the direction of Barbizon.
Their herdsman under the silver-gray sky
bears the euphonious name of
Théodore Rousseau.

But there are other gardens here.
They always seem to begin with a few vertical lines,
extended, as is fitting, beyond the picture,
just as the rain has its origin high above us
and its end point, in fact, under our bootsoles.
Thus are gardens created from infinity!
Everything stems from it, everything's filtered
through tribal trunks, all descent makes
verticals, everything gets stripes, the day breaks
up and down.

Those sharp angles—where do they come from?
And the swallows—what do they mean?
There are so many questions here, so quick
that they're nearly invisible.
They rush through the air catercorner
and vanish somewhere near the eavestroughs.

The cows have no answers.
The cows are unfathomable.
They won't be allowed to stay here.
They make the landscape dated,
but the memory of them still hangs in the air.
Can't have, either,
the people rowing on the river in blue-and-white
striped shirts. Nor their underwear
which on certain laundry days hangs on the drying racks
far into the darkness. Only now
can the river flow through the pictures.

"Painters need the light of day,"
says the man in the charcuterie,
"but poets probably work best at night."
That's why they have balconies near the moonlight.
A painter can ignore the night.
It applies its shadow to the panels on its own
and becomes the sum of all colors.

Grez-sur-Loing, May 1996

On Average

Memory is as red as a Sunday morning
when no one has ventured past the long building yet
so as not to disturb the people dozing there
in silent chairs inside the barber shop.
Memory is their hair, which grows imperceptibly
to replace what has slowly turned white and been swept into piles on the
    floor.

All of that lives behind the red,
so far away that only music can take us there unharmed

through the reflections from enormous cities, fireplace cities.
We pass five years of our lives in dreams
while the all-night radio station keeps playing. On average.
In his sleep the barber trims
the moon into a square.

The question is, to be purely grammatical:
How many tenses can we live in at once?
The answer's in this glowing red—infinitely many,
all meaningless if we aren't in them—
cities stripped down to their skeletons
in a walking boogie-woogie, airy rooms
in gigantic buildings that are collapsing
or haven't yet collapsed.

October 2001

Squares

The square is the basis of everything
we load up with litter and curios.

The square is the tabletop
where small buckets of blue-black mussels are set out,
wine bottles, glasses, white plates, the bread basket, then the cheeses.
They all have their own shapes
yet they're inscribed in the square
like the cigarettes
in your shiny case.

The square is the tablecloth
the shapeless conversation drifts across.
We're gray-haired now,

but still the discussion will continue for a while
with undiminished strength.
Neither of us will remember what was said,
only that it signified just then.
A faint sadness does not exclude a certain esprit.
The former remains, the latter disappears
like our tobacco smoke above the square
of the restaurant's patio.

The last square on the board is always black.

The square is the nighttime plaza
you cross
in your black and violet shoes.

October 2005

Image after Image after Image

To Olle Kåks

1.

So many years, and what they've laid down is a womanly being
resting on a branch, soft parts twisted into a flower of skin,
an endless repetition of swallows, cat's paws, leaf-buds, woolen mittens,
    shoelaces, knapsacks,
an Ardennes cart-horse with such heavy horseshoes, good luck but heavy.

Resting on a branch, soft parts twisted into a flower of skin,
and even so there remained a black torso, unexplained,
an Ardennes cart-horse with such heavy horseshoes, good luck but heavy.
For certain thoughts a ship made of dung is the suitable vehicle.

And even so there remained a black torso, unexplained.
Waste products guarantee that life will continue.
For certain thoughts a ship made of dung is the suitable vehicle.
You have to feel that you're alive—even through your shame.

Waste products guarantee that life will continue.
There's an orienteering map to the unknown. A scythe is rusting there.
You have to feel that you're alive—even through your shame.
So don't wake him, the one who's snored his way into unshakability,
    leaning forward.

2.

There's an orienteering map to the unknown. A scythe is rusting there.
We're inscribed in a giant triangle.
So don't wake him, the one who's snored his way into unshakability,
    leaning forward.
He's writing his name across the whole wall.

We're inscribed in a giant triangle.
He gives in to a primitive need for luxury, the origin of all décor.
He's writing his name across the whole wall.
The peacock feathers plaster the room with eyes that look in all
    directions.

He gives in to a primitive need for luxury, the origin of all décor.
The triangle is open. From there life can squeeze out.
The peacock feathers plaster the room with eyes that look in all
    directions.
I imagine we can see with all these eyes.

The triangle is open. From there life can squeeze out,
wolfskin, birch-bark, swan's neck, serpent, paving stone, gold, peat-litter.
I imagine we can see with all these eyes
in a burial chamber of earth and stone, gazing into ourselves.

3.

Wolfskin, birch-bark, swan's neck, serpent, paving stone, gold, peat-litter.
All that stuff is scattered now, we left it
in a burial chamber of earth and stone, gazing into ourselves.
The water rises around us and becomes the world's largest lake.

All that stuff is scattered now, we left it.
Maybe it will keep drifting around as flotsam.
The water rises around us and becomes the world's largest lake,
Lake Superior, a month of shimmering water.

Maybe it will keep drifting around as flotsam,
a floating symphony orchestra, flapping wing-beats inside a gladstone
    bag.
Lake Superior, a month of shimmering water.
A lonesome tuba is walking around in the grass.

A floating symphony orchestra, flapping wing-beats inside a gladstone
    bag.
The word *bird* became an image, the image bird a word.
A lonesome tuba is walking around in the grass.
We had no plans to reinvent hieroglyphics.

4.

The word *bird* became an image, the image bird a word.
The sun paints the shutters yellow, behind them an ocean swarming with
    stars.
We had no plans to reinvent hieroglyphics.
Our fear of the wild and freely roving inhibits us.

The sun paints the shutters yellow, behind them an ocean swarming with
    stars.
Darkness in motion is fire, breaking out, rolling back to itself.
Our fear of the wild and freely roving inhibits us
and that's the whole truth, right now that's the whole truth.

Darkness in motion is fire, breaking out, rolling back to itself,
a blackthorn bush blazing with white flowers,
and that's the whole truth, right now that's the whole truth.
You can find it in the middle of a flower, inside a fossilized sign.

So many years, and what they've laid down is a womanly being,
a blackthorn bush blazing with white flowers.
You can find it in the middle of a flower, inside a fossilized sign.
Turning back wasn't what I had in mind. No, here is where I was heading.

The Burning Child

It isn't fire that consumes. It is
fear of the flare-up, especially the nighttime one
in which the past's humiliations won't reveal themselves
and therefore can't be burned up.
If you turn the light on fast you may just glimpse
a few small beings in outdated clothes
scurrying back behind the gray curtain. Was that all?
The irreducible element that does not burn is guilt,
but guilt owed to whom and how to pay it off
other than with the black banknotes that insomnia counterfeits

in order to finance not a new birth, perhaps
but a new spring day in childhood when memory lies ahead of me
and sets the fire-alarm boxes aglow.
Just as well that I'm not tall enough to reach them:
could never resist the strange temptation to smash the little window,
pull the handle and run away in a cacophony of horns
and blaring brass bells.
And yet it happens. Entirely on its own!
The firehouse throws open its doors
and there stands the fire engine newly washed,
bright red and with shiny brass fittings,
soapy water sparkling down toward the storm sewer.

The firemen put on their helmets
and drive a few laps around the block.
In this daydream all alarms are false.
It's just the sun reflecting off the windows.
No fire anywhere, not a fire in the whole city.

But the fear is still there. Fear of what?
That something will catch fire behind the closed door,

something that's been left behind. And it would all be my fault.
A child is running around in there, burning.
No one can hear him
until I become his scream.

1940

We can call the place Sundsvall, we can call
this month June; "In a hospital room,"
we can hum. "West Norrland county"
says my passport for all time, 1940.
I stared up at the sky so long
that my eyes turned blue. And what glided past
up there—was that clouds? No, clouds aren't green.
It must have been tree branches, I realize now.
My first summer and my first thoughts,
not words yet but leaves and wads of cloud
and a smell of sawdust, women's faces leaning over me
with red lipstick-mouths, and behind them
stood the brick building, thinking.

Everything was newborn and came to me
as questions, as air, as nothing.
There's someone who is me, still
"with his head in the clouds." So much happens there.
Everything wants to be born in a child, colors without names
but with many meanings. The ocean too
searched for its color and found it. Something dark,
it was a memory, something to find again on waking.
Stay with me always, don't leave me here
beside the grayest of oceans,
the grayest of wars,
which no thought could ever.... And yet:
Before I was born I was already yearning to be here.
I really did want to exist,
even if I often cried.

1941 (Judarn Lake)

In this place long ago there lived a woman.
The only task she had
was to name the lakes.
On each shore she sat quietly listening,
looked out across the nameless surface,
slowly rocking, the lake and the woman
both rocking slowly.
After a time the name was ready.
She uttered it over the surface of the water.
Then she went off to another lake.
Her job was done.
The lake purls and murmurs,
trying to pronounce its name.

I've never seen anyone bathing here
but I have rarely been here on moonlit nights
when the blackness attracts
bathers descended to the forest lake from the moon,
motionless and silvered by its paleness—borrowed, re-borrowed
and never returned.

For months their clothing remains on the shore.
A patient escaped from Beckomberga
walks bloated and screaming under the trees.
She has seen the whole thing,
but no one believes her.
She sits down at the shore.
The lake remembers her. Together they rock, pale,
pale with borrowed light.

1944 (Beckomberga)

The snow is so deep that the mailman has called in sick.
It's made to order for the hospital grounds.
I'm sure I could lift it on my fingertips.
That's how easy it is to lift snow.

I'm sitting on a sled.
"Hitler! Hitler!" He's there too
in a madwoman's imagination.
She walks by and shouts:
"Goddamned brat, I'll kill you!"
My heart pounds all the way up the stairs.
Papa's standing in the hall in heavy military furs.
There's a smell of war.
In the movies shown in the pistachio-green brick building
the horses are galloping shadows.
I go up to the screen and pet them
and the patients laugh.
A real horse has a stronger smell.
Shaggy and brown, it stands in front of a cart full of frozen sand.
It's munching oats from a feed bag.
I run under its belly.
That's how small I am.

I never sang in a voice pure as snow.
I'm licking a snowball and singing anyway.
People walk around with snow on their caps
outside the fence on Vassvägen.
The buses are the reddest ones I've seen.
No crayon is as red as that.
The hospital wrapped in white.
There's someone there who's called a "manager."
He takes care of everything.

1948

My brother's sitting high in the linden tree, the tall one
near the wall. He can't get down.
My sister has blond braids and a pink ribbon in her hair.
A girl arrives from Germany.
She has dark braids. She's crying.
My father puts on his bicycle clips.
He rides to Odengatan 9 with his hat and his briefcase.
Something dark that's happened somewhere else must be understood.
When the streetlights come on we have to run home.
I stand panting in the foyer.
My mother's in the kitchen. She looks sad.
She's dicing carrots.
My brother's lying in bed eating gooseberry fool with a teaspoon
to make it last longer.
He lies in bed for a year and eats and eats
but only gets skinnier.
I lie on my stomach on the floor and draw a war that never ends.
Something dark that must be understood
is between the lampposts. Something dark seeps into me
and becomes a spirited lifelong despair.
There are orange cubes to be eaten cooked.
There is a man in a dark overcoat and a fur hat.
He goes out skating in the evening darkness.
His path would be hidden from me
if it weren't for the graceful movements of his glowing cigar.
There's white smoke above his head.
Columns of smoke from chimneys rise straight up over the roofs.
They are the houses' frozen souls,
visible perhaps because of the moonlight,
perhaps because of something else
that will never be revealed to me.

1949 (The Erica Foundation's Institute for Child Psychology)

The idea was that you built your world in a sandbox.
Each toy had its hidden meaning,
and where you placed it. Whether the sand was moist or dry
was also significant—you could choose.
What looked like pictures on the walls
were in fact spy-holes
behind which the psychologists were making their notes.
Detection was what these pictures were about,
not the subjects they portrayed.
The child was the true subject,
his play and the impressions it left in the sand.
He's sitting on the edge of the sandbox
and gripping a small piece of picket fence.
This represents his inner state, although imperfectly,
the way a tin roof awkwardly mirrors the sky
and gives it its own tired, corrugated form.
Now he's turning his gaze toward me.
He sees this far
but doesn't notice that I'm observing him.
All he sees is a painted landscape
that portrays my childhood.

1951

To think that we had so many knives! Fruit knives, of course.
It was a middle-class home. And to think people actually threw them
but missed. Everyone's sure I'm mistaken
when I say that my brother had a knife quivering in his forehead
as he staggered down the steps to the astonishment
of twenty-three newly minted child psychologists.
But the scar is still there

like the forces that make a pointed object whizz through the air
in a bedroom to which four kids have been banished
with each an apple and an orange as consolation
while the dark humming of the psychologists
rises from below, an indistinct murmur
across the parquet floor, under the brass chandelier, between the
    bookshelves
and the flowered 1940s easy chairs. I don't understand much
about this, mainly recall the stage props
and the nights
when four kids made the house breathe heavily behind the roll-down
    shades
that blocked the stars from us, their blue-white scars
not yet healed by bleached-out spring skies.

In the house across the way lived a man with a glass eye
who sold miracle-working homeopathic sugar pills.
With well-aimed charges of buckshot he wiped out
the crows on our roof
so they wouldn't fly off the next day
and discover what was going on in the outside world.

1952

Does history stop because the history teacher is dead
or does it move on—watched by a farmer
who looks up from his plow—as a motley procession
under fluttering banners, preferably accompanied by music?
And all for the sake of a pretty but treacherous queen!
Or as a caravan of black ants through the sugar,
headed up by Sven Hedin. Through his large binoculars
we saw deserts of pebbles or marble chips.

It was all, we understood then, a matter of magnification—
of enlarging ideals, heroism, the adventure itself
and with the larger format, sharpness was reduced.
All this was taught in the photography club that met
in a small darkroom above the map collection
where sloppy tubs of fixer could give
even newly snapped pictures a "historical" patina.
With the passage of years they grow clearer and clearer,
I might almost say more contemporary.

It's the cruelties that make the past clear
and they're forever repeated by those who remember their history.
The rest of us try timidly to get along with it,
surrounded by it in the schoolyard
unable to escape the ring
of half-forgotten details: scuffed toe-caps,
darned socks, being tripped or kicked in the shins.
Memory blots out the wrongs
but at night the images regain their sharpness.

Though color is a later phase.
Back then a gray film lay over even "the black board"
where "Do not erase!" was always written in the lower right corner.

But someone always wet the eraser nonetheless
and wiped away everything but those three words
because history had to be obliterated all the time
and make room for us so our motley bands,
bewildered and historyless, could run out
onto the stone-dead gravel court.

1953

It isn't everyone who grew up in a psychiatric house
with a green sofa that reeked of neuroses
though the place was forever being aired out
even on cold winter days when the bullfinches
sat bleeding in the bare apple trees.
It isn't everyone who knows what it means
to sit on a parapet
high up and without a flyboard
although you can see others flying by,
some of them even sitting up in their beds.

The fear of falling gives rise to such fantasies.
Nonetheless you fall each night into the cellar,
that little room full of cells inside your forehead
where murmuring voices are constantly drowned out
by the ventilation system that hums and whirs
but never gets serious about dispersing
the deep feeling of guilt,
stronger than all visual impressions.

Was the only salvation to live in reverse?
The psychiatrist himself sat lost in thought
behind his desk.
You quickly learned never to tell your dreams.
They only deepened his pondering and made him
walk in circles with his hands folded on his back.

The fragments of dream that ended up in sketchbooks
were filed in stacks in the attic,
waiting for what? Waiting for the day
when they would merge
into a decipherable whole, and when the guilt

whose surface tension was increasing all the time
would explode and I would rocket up backwards
from the deep end like a high diver
and stand there, brightly lit,
completely dry and completely true,
for the truth is almost always naked.
This scared me more
than the voices murmuring below.

1954

By New Year strong feelings were already in play
and once we'd bought a blockbuster that big
we damn well couldn't waste it
just because the fuse had gone out
a few millimeters from the rocket.
Our ears rang all the way to the verge of spring
when no one cared anymore about who had won the snowball war
and the crocuses peeked out, yellow and bluish violet,
just the way first love is experienced
by those who haven't yet felt its tremendous weight.
I stood in the dusk and spoke
to a closed lit window on the second floor.

Maybe she would notice me after all
if I succeeded in blowing up the Public Works Department's big blue sand
    container
outside her house with gunpowder from the cartridges I'd found
in the wake of army maneuvers in Kvarnback Forest.
I emptied the powder into a paper bag,
lit one corner and threw it in
under the container's lid.
I thought the box would lift off the ground
and detonate at a height of 20 meters
but it just went *pffft*.
That's how a lack of compression
can weaken the effects of the most powerful feelings.
Across the empty cartridge shells
I blew breathless tunes
like "After You've Gone."

1956

So much of this happened
in basements, in thick woolen sweaters, in B major
but with strong passages in minor. On the outskirts.
That's where we were from
but our thoughts had wings like the pigeons
and like them tried to find urban quarters
where the life of the spirit was more shaded, fluttering
over stone walls heavy with history. The shadow-play of thoughts
exposed what words concealed, that no love is as strong
as the one that goes unrequited. A gentle drizzle
fell over the bike rack. I remember everything
from inside the rain.

No one said it more plainly than the clarinetist
in his solo in "Creole Love Call"
with Duke Ellington's Orchestra. Literally
heartrending. For those who love each other music
is just the background. For the one who's no longer loved
it's everything. He hears it from inside the drizzle
up the street and down again. Who has the right
in this context to poke fun at Pathetic images:
a heart pierced by a spindle
on a rotating platter.
Then notes rise up
which the shadows can dance to; the others' shadows.

1957 (Metamorphoses)

The sunlight slants in
through the classroom window,
starts glinting off the Latin teacher's glasses.
Coctilibus muris cinxisse Semiramis urbem.
Walled city of Semiramis, sun
through the crack in the wall, sun
that glints on the pen-point, warms
the ink in the inkwell.

Take the pen and write:
Whoever sneaks out at night
will find only a veil torn to shreds.
Those who seek love
will redden the fruit of the trees
with their blood
or after their union
will be transformed into dragons
that can only hiss at each other
in a Hell furnished with butterfly chairs
where the portable radio is playing "You Are My Destiny."

How does transformation go? As a rule
from something febrile and fleeting
to something slow and thoughtful.
From panting with desire, shirt flapping,
to becoming a stone, a tree, a green coulisse,
and like the thing you chased,
being reunited with the unfathomable.
These green leaves
were once the thoughts of high school students.

All fossilizing is motion, all motion fossilizing.
The white lilacs on the teacher's desk. That's how they looked:
the petticoats the girls wore
starched with sugary soda.
The ardent light of early summer
shows it's examination day.
Now the play will be performed again, and we,
a collection of seedy characters,
will assume the roles of gods and goddesses.

I'm the one playing the wall.

One day it will be split
by the notes of a flute
as piercingly lonesome
as only a despised god can be.

1958 (Miss Setterdahl's Art School)

I wore a green corduroy jacket
with discreet spots of oil paint in coelin blue, my favorite color.
The nude model was reading *Doctor Zhivago* by that year's Nobel Prize
    winner
but had only gotten to page 98:
"At that moment he realized more clearly than ever before
that art constantly, stubbornly, deals with two things:
It always meditates on death
and thus always creates life."

Wasn't it actually just the reverse?
The model put on her dressing gown, lit a cigarette
and walked around scrutinizing one after another
the wet canvases firmly fastened to their easels with thumbtacks.
Had even one of us succeeded in capturing the luster
that hovered near her skin? No,
in every case a hint of death had crept into the colors.

Later, over coffee, someone put the question:
Will any of us ever find
that tinge of life
that only certain artists in each century capture?
We sat in a row along the tablecloth of shelving paper
as in Leonardo's *Last Supper*
with coffee cups and cheese sandwiches in our hands.
Every face, embarrassed, turned away:
Not me. Not me. Not me.

1962 (K4 in Umeå)

We were here to defend this forest
and become a part of this green
that our tents and uniforms clumsily mimicked.
The forest would not be fooled.
Spruce branches slapped us in the face when we rode past,
tree trunks scraped against our knees.
If someone fell out of the saddle he inevitably landed
with his back on a pine root.

In the winter we dressed up as snow.
To be invisible and then deadly
was the point.
To obliterate ourselves
so we could later obliterate others.
The green forest wouldn't acknowledge us.
The white snow did not love us.
We were Norrland's last dragoons.
Dressed in white, snowblind, camouflaged as snow
we guarded a whiteness
we would never be part of
in the country from Tavelsjö to Täfteå.

You Sleep More Deeply than the Sea

Henrik Larm (1980–2001)

You left a party you weren't enjoying,
went down to the shore at midnight,
undressed and swam out
into a body of water as large and as gray
as a dream you remember you dreamt
but don't remember.

The sea's longing for us is so strong,
and you had drifted out to sea before and returned,
each time with a laugh. You were the kind
who often drifted off, whatever "off" might mean.
You always discovered something there, felt at home
in the gliding motion itself, as in your boyhood hockey games
before anyone had learned to brake with his skates
so you had to keep going forward
until you collided with something or someone
and tumbled down laughing.

I'm sitting in an unfurnished apartment five flights up
among stacks of unopened cartons.
"I won't let you be dead anymore,"
I heard Karin Bellman read through the hum of a jazz club.
I wish I could have written that line
in the hissing summer rain that's missing your laugh,
missing your laugh, missing your laugh.

I won't let you be dead anymore.
I haven't yet learned the language of the dead
which writes its glyphs tonight in what I see outside
—the heavy Jugend-style building with its copper helmet,

people who move behind the windows and later do not move
as the pale blue TV light drowns
apartment after annihilated apartment.

Ich weiss nicht, was soll es bedeuten

Do we have to know what it means
when a tranquil sorrow fills the room
as the music box plays "Lorelei," first energetically
but later slowing down, only to stop at last
in the middle of the melody? Of course it's a comfort to know
that the closing bars still live inside it
with their melancholy among the cogs.
They haven't been obliterated. Have just gone back
to another time and another place
in a mechanical universe
where consciousness is complex but poor of spirit
because it's been formed of the senses
and cast in bronze. It's so shiny
that it actually *chimes!* This exact melody
rings out from a Glockenturm across a city
where tranquillity lies heavy as the snow on the roofs
since all those gripped by passion have been snuffed out,
snuffed out in the dark river.

"Sweet, sweet and long, the song the siren sang."

But the stars there seem made of sugar,
precisely of sugar, cute and artificial,
not at all like the black light bulb
that has attained perfection here.
It gives our windows a shiny blackness
so they're easily mistaken for the blackboards
where our life stories will be written.
What name shall we give this dark electricity?
I'm not saying, but I know that it changes everything—
the season, the setting, the temperature, yes the mood itself—
and leads us back to ourselves

like the subway trains that find their way home at night
along the tracks of current, a series of cars,
each one scrawled over with its own darkness.

Departure

The biggest problem is not
to get the sailing ship into the bottle.
The biggest problem is after that
to get the wind to fill the sails.
It isn't done in a day,
but when it happens
it's the work of a moment.

That's when it begins.
That's when it ends.
It's the same thing.
You are my last love.

We are at a party where some walk straight through us,
others stand aligned in profile against the water.
In the background a large brick building, ignited by the sun.
Boats pass before it and those who stand on the shore
resemble the relatives of someone who's just departed.
This takes place every year.
The guests have remained here the whole time.
We are the only ones who've been somewhere else
and it's hard for them to bear this.
We are the story they tell one another.
"*Calm* is a good word," someone says, but for what?

Remembered images of what doesn't exist yet
can help us, if we miss it keenly enough.
I lay my ear on your belly and hear
the babble of all the children we can never have.
They are here and they aren't here. Today is tomorrow
and they are setting out in small boats that have slipped out of their
    bottles.

Water and sky are so transparent
that we can see all the way down to the southern Baltic
west of the Midsjö Banks,
no, even farther.

Infectious Disease Ward, Sundsvall Hospital

Strange that we didn't feel the infection approaching
past the harbor's warehouses, through the stone quarter
up from the spruce-covered heights,
and that the fever rose so fast while the snowfall cooled the streets.
The chills shook the Comfort Hotel all through the night.
Thanks for plundering the hotel's supply of linens
when we kept having to change the sheets and the soaked pillowcases.
    Thanks
for disregarding me and turning up in the doorway
with two ruddy ambulance attendants in thick coveralls.

Has Waldteufel ever tried to put into music the ethereal melancholy of
    hospital wards?
The music station doesn't say in its crackling box near the pillow.
It's as if the snow wanted to put reminders of itself in here
in all this whiteness, right down to the sallow cream cheese on the
    breakfast toast.
Doctors, nurses, and aides glide through the ward in a graceful ballet,
remote-controlled by our favorite choreographer, Margaretha Åsberg of
    Dansens hus.
Then you're standing there in my room again in your suede greatcoat
down to your ankles, like the people Waldteufel composed for
in his charming arabesques for skaters' swooping blades.
Here love is furnished with surprising props:
a plastic bag with four Ingrid Marie apples, a "Fruit and Almond" choco-
    late cake,
the *Sundsvall Daily* with a review of a feverish performance,
and paper tissues to remind me of the snow that you've come from

and that we will soon return to, watching it billow
across the airport's deserted runways that try
to look like they're in Archangelsk, out of all proportion

to the few shivering propeller planes.
And we will travel on in a fever
that seems to be permanently ours, vibrating under our clothes.

Tegnérgatan

The question How long can it go on snowing
can't be answered yet. A few hours ago
two men in blue riding a cherry picker chopped snow and icicles
off the eavestroughs across the street. Now the snow is driving again
while they sit in the café on the corner
and grow frustrated trying to finish up the brown sauce with their knives.
The bicycles' black skeletons in the drifts
make me ponder without fear
how mortality is something that goes on all the time
and remind me that I earn my living from it.

On Tegnér Street I am always two, until you come into the foyer
and we are one again. Was there a time when we didn't
know each other? We must go back there
together, visit the streets, remember
the old security codes, peek into the stairwells.
There the people we used to be walk past on the sidewalks
craning upward the whole while,
afraid that sheets of old ice will crash down on them.
They're upset that we pay them no mind.

The vibrations are noticeable throughout the building.
A picture has already fallen to the floor
and a free but lost soul has escaped.
Another picture is a framed storm
that casts its darkness over us
but not between us. Really we should
divide it down the middle and take each our dark half. No,
we're both incapable of living in half a storm.
In the thunder we lean closer to each other.

We lie together on the bed, warm as the snow
while people leave us little by little
until we are the dusk above the city, completely still.

Rugosa Roses

We saw the heavy trees near the parking lot dancing in the
    thundershower
and realized that the person who died would be following us on our trip.
The letters kept arriving
but we could no longer open them.
On both sides of the highway the cornfields stretched out,
so vast that we would never find ourselves in them.
At 4 o'clock, precisely 4 o'clock each morning
the crazy runaway rooster woke up alarmed
and let loose among the nettles,
and half-asleep people muttered: "I'll kill you!"
The sky was improbably blue, soundless and blue
but our friend at the black lake had seen
the old airforce general sitting in his chair in dress whites
and he had said: "There's nothing to be afraid of."

So weird that neither of us noticed
how quickly everything changed. Today it's a hundred years from now
and we are back in the white cottage by the shore
where the shadows of roes pass across the property at night.
They eat the rugosa roses and melt away in the dawn.
Is that still us sitting there on the shore
in shirts blazing white with sunshine? We don't know.
Maybe all our shadows too have melted
into a story about love among wrinkled roses
good for groundcover and hardy even in poor soil,
an elaborately detailed tapestry
where no threads have grown worn, no colors have faded,
and you look up in your characteristic way
with lively eyes, green as the garden table,
exactly as no photographer has managed to capture you.
But the rose hedge has grown tall and dense.

It covers the whole house, and we're the only ones who know about
the dark room inside
where the white flower flows out.

Epilogue

What was the question? I don't remember,
but in any case the answer is: Love.
And the boy wakes up.
The flames have stopped licking at the walls and roof.
The smell of smoke remains, but it comes from
the pipe that's gone out. He is sixty-two now.
The doorknobs seize up but after a while
it's possible to coax the doors open.
The shoes in the foyer are entirely too small.
That's how long he slept inside the fire.

We call this weather gray
until we've taken the time to discover the bricks
glowing through the buildings' crumbling plaster.
Silhouettes of the chimneys, inquisitors
with unlimited power, blackened to their limits.
They no longer have anything to accuse me of.
The boy sits at the kitchen table and draws.
He wants me to leave him in peace.
Later he'll come to me with the paper
and show me what he saw
in the middle of the fire.

Notes

NOTES

(I have translated the notes credited to Gunnar Harding and have supplied the others, sometimes on the basis of information provided by Harding. —RG)

It Is Evening When You Turn Back   p. 38
   "stranger, as you pass by …": from a very common epitaph that is found in many variants. One example, from the grave of Abner T. Shaw in the cemetery at Shaw House outside Nashville, TN, begins "Behold stranger as you pass by, / as you are now so once was I." (http://abnertshawhouse.com /cemetery.html)

The Train in the Background Is the Rock Island Line   p. 41
   "Anselm Hollo": American poet of Finnish descent (1934–2013). GH: a close friend, who starting in the mid-1960s furnished me with hard-to-obtain books and information about contemporary American poetry. We co-edited the 1979 anthology *Modern Swedish Poetry* (University of Minnesota Press).

On the Way to Little Big Horn   p. 45
   "Little Big Horn": GH: the place in Montana where in 1876 General Custer led the 7th Cavalry into death in a foolhardy attack on Sitting Bull's encampment.

Rebel without a Cause   p. 46
   Directed by Nicholas Ray (1955).

20 July 1969—1944   p. 49
   GH: The American moon-landing by the Apollo Project took place twenty-five years to the day after Count Stauffenberg's unsuccessful attempt to assassinate Hitler. The lunar landing craft was called *The Eagle,* and the words "*The Eagle* has landed" were the crew's message to the Earth after the successful landing.
   The Wolf's Lair: the name of Hitler's headquarters in Rastenburg, East Prussia (now Kętrzyn in Poland), where the attempted assassination took place.

Für Janet Persson   p. 53
   Bildjournalen: a popular magazine for teenagers (especially girls) in the 1950s and 60s. It featured movie stars, pop singers, horoscopes, advice columns, etc.

I Decide to Take Up the Battle against *Bonnier's Literary Magazine*   p. 57
   Albert Bonnier is the name of one of the largest and most prestigious publishing houses in Sweden; the firm also published the journal referred to in this poem's title.

Grandpa and the Little Old Ladies in Leksand   p. 66

GH: Leksand is not a town, but what we call a "socken," a parish, population 13,000, situated in Dalarna (Dalecarlia) where Dalälven (the Dalälven River) flows out of Lake Siljan. My maternal grandfather was a schoolteacher and church organist there, and my grandmother was the librarian. Dalecarlia is a center for traditional Swedish folk culture.

"This blesséd day...": the first words of the medieval hymn referred to near the beginning of the poem.

"J. O. Wallin": poet and bishop, editor of the old Swedish hymnal and author of many of the hymns in it.

Europe—A Winter Journey   p. 71

"The Ghetto Swingers": GH: In the Theresienstadt concentration camp there was actually a jazz band with this name, under the direction of Friček Weiss. When the Red Cross got permission in 1944 to inspect this camp, which the Nazis tried to present as a "model camp," the Ghetto Swingers held a concert. The very next day, the band members were being sent to Auschwitz. Friček Weiss rejected an offer to play in the camp orchestra there and instead voluntarily accompanied his family to death in the gas chambers.

"the *Tirpitz*": one of the Third Reich's most powerful battleships, sister ship to the *Bismarck*. Commissioned in 1941; used mainly in Norwegian waters to attack Allied convoys to Russia; repeatedly attacked; finally sunk by British bombers on 12 November 1944.

"Westerplatte": a Polish fortress outside Danzig (Gdansk) that went on fighting in 1939 while the rest of Poland fell into German and Russian hands.

Cape Farewell   p. 79

This poem was not in fact included in *Ballader* (1975). Harding omitted it because it had recently appeared in a widely circulated anthology, *Dikten finns överallt: Svensk poesi idag* [Poems Are Everywhere: Swedish Poetry Today], ed. Tobias Berggren and Theodor Kallifatides (Stockholm: FIBs Lyrikklub, 1973). But in subsequent volumes of his selected poems, Harding placed the poem with the ones from *Ballader.*

"the flag of the Union": the flag of the Norway-Sweden union (1814–1905).

"*undir Grœnlandsjöklum í vík nokkurri við sandmöl*": literally, "under Greenland's glacier in a certain bay near gravel." From Haukr Erlendsson, *Flóamanna saga*, chap. 23. See *Íslendinga sögur og pættir*, ed. Bragi Halldórsson, Jón Torfason, Sverrir Tómasson, Örnólfur Thorsson (Reykjavik: Svart á Hvítu, 1987), 1:748 (my thanks to Zoe Borovsky for locating the source and translating the phrase). For the rest of the episode about Thorgils, see 1:750.

Harding recalls having come across these passages in Fridtjof Nansen's account of his exploration of Greenland. They can be found in the original Norwegian edition of *Nansen, Paa ski over Grønland: En skildring af den Norske Grønlands-ekspedition 1888–89* (Kristiania: Aschehoug, 1890), 251–2. The original English version includes the shipwreck, but not Thorgils's nursing of his son: *The First Crossing of Greenland,* trans. Hubert Majendie Gepp (London: Longmans, Green, 1890), 1:275. In a note in the Norwegian edition, Nansen asserts that earlier Norwegian translations of jöklum as "isbjerge" (iceberg) are completely unjustified. Given this concern for accurate translation, it is worth noting that he renders "í vík nokkurri við sandmöl" as "i en vik ved en sandig strandbred" (which Gepp translates as "in an inlet which had sandy shores"). This would seem to pit the explorer's knowledge of the topography against the lexicographers' knowledge of words in texts.

Elsewhere Nansen concludes that the story of Thorgils's shipwreck is "not very credible," but may have "a historical kernel." See Nansen, *In Northern Mists: Arctic Exploration in Early Times,* trans. Arthur G. Chater (London: Heinemann, 1911), 1:280. This is a translation of *Nord i tåkeheimen: utforskningen av jordens nordlige strøk i tidlige tider* (Kristiania: Dybwad, 1911).

Lasse-Maja at Carlsten Fortress   p. 88
Carlsten Fortress, in Marstrand, about 25 miles (40 km) northeast of Gothenburg, was built from 1658 to 1860 by convicts sentenced to "Marstrand hard labor," a special punishment found in the Swedish Statute Book in that period. The master thief Lasse-Maja (Lars Larsson Molin) was imprisoned in the fortress from 1813 until he was pardoned in 1838; accounts of his exploits made popular reading. His nickname reflected the fact that he had often operated in female disguise (Lasse is a common nickname for the man's name Lars; Maja is a woman's name).

Grandma Grandpa and the Memory of Jenny Wilkas   p. 91
"Kreuger & Toll": GH: a manufacturer of matches, the most solid enterprise in Sweden in the 1920s, one would have thought. When Kreuger shot himself in Paris the firm and the whole Swedish economy collapsed. My paternal grandfather lost all his money and his estate.

"Covering the ground / on all fours again": GH: based on a line in an unpublished poem by Anselm Hollo about our horseback-riding expeditions in Iowa: "walking / the earth again   on all fours."

Danny's Dream   p. 94
GH: Lasse Gullin's recording of this ballad in 1954 constitutes the most highly charged five minutes in the history of Swedish jazz.

The Black Death   p. 98
GH: This is how the Black Death came to Scandinavia, at least according to the legend: an English ship whose whole crew had died went aground outside Bergen. It was loaded with cloth; people stole it, and so the contagion was spread.

Buddy Bolden's Original Jass & Ragtime Band   p. 107
GH: An essay on Buddy Bolden, the first jazz trumpeter, appears in my book *Kreol* [Creole] (1991).
There are two published versions of this poem. The original version appeared in *Blommor till James Dean* [Flowers for James Dean] (1969); a revised version appeared in Harding's second volume of selected poems, *Överallt där vinden finns* [Wherever the Wind Is Blowing] (1993). I prefer the original version and, with Harding's permission, have based my translation on that text.

Davenport Blues   p. 110
GH: Bix Beiderbecke is discussed in my collection of essays *Den trådlösa fantasin* [The Wireless Imagination] (1978).

Bunk Johnson in New Iberia   p. 113
GH: According to legend (and himself) Bunk Johnson was the last survivor of the first jazz band, Buddy Bolden's band. In the thirties he lost his teeth, couldn't play the trumpet anymore, and retired to the small town of New Iberia, Louisiana, where he took various jobs—among others truck-driving for the local Tabasco factory. Poor and forgotten, he was rediscovered by the jazz historian Bill Russell in the early forties and made his first record and his incredible comeback in 1942. This is a major event in American cultural history!

Persephone   p. 130
GH: Some of the imagery in this poem was inspired by the famous Magritte painting in which the man in a dark coat is inside the contours of the woman.

Åkersbodarna   p. 133
Åkersbodarna ['o-kers-ˌbü-där-nä] is the name of a small village in Leksand parish.

Créole   p. 135
GH: In 1981 I spent a month in Martinique to study Creole culture.
Arawaks: the indigenous people of the West Indies.

History-painting   p. 138

GH: The first section of this poem refers to my childhood at Beckomberga Mental Hospital in Bromma, western Stockholm, where my father was a doctor. We lived inside the fence of the hospital area. My grandmother had a small house, "Ekeberg," in Ljungskile on the Swedish west coast (see the poem "Grandma Grandpa and the Memory of Jenny Wilkas"), where I spent many of my childhood summers. In her attic there were heaped a great many old things: albums for postcards from the turn of the century, and an old chest packed when her brother Arthur was sent to the mental hospital in Gothenburg in 1910 (he stayed there until his death in the 1970s). It contained his clothes, but also the last letter from Natalia (the excerpt from it in part 2 of the poem is authentic). He had been in love with her, the daughter of a priest, but her parents wouldn't let them marry, as he was only a blacksmith. This event caused the breakdown that led to his life-long mental illness and hospitalization—at least, according to my grandmother. As Arthur was very interested in history and studied it at the asylum, I filled the poem with references to Swedish history.

The Star-diver   p. 151

This poem, "Stjärndykaren," is the opening poem in the Swedish volume that bears the same title, but its final section, under the title "Stjärndykaren / (fragment till en epilog)," is printed separately as the closing piece in the book. Here the final section appears together with the main body of the poem.

The Gate Coin   p. 156

The poem's title ("Grindslanten") refers to a well-known painting by August Malmström (1829–1901), which depicts a group of boys scrambling for a coin presumably tossed by a carter who has passed the gate they've opened for him (the cart can be made out in the distance).

Adonais   p. 158

GH: "Adonais" is the title of Shelley's elegy for his fellow poet Keats, in which he freely embroiders the myth of Adonis. Shelley wrote the poem in Pisa in 1821. The house where he lived was badly damaged during World War II, but remains as a ruin. Viareggio is where Shelley's body washed ashore in 1822 after his sailing accident.

Guarding the Air   p. 161

The title of this poem, "Luftbevakning," refers to a civil defense activity common during World War II and variously called "air-raid patrol," "plane spotting," "aircraft recognition," etc. I have chosen to translate the constituent elements of the title word in a way that I think conveys Harding's play on its meaning.

The first sentence of section 4— "Här är landet som inte, är landet som inte, / landet som blir." ("Here is the land that never, is the land that never, / the land that becomes")—is an unmistakable reference to the opening of a well-known poem by Edith Södergran (1892–1923), "Landet som icke är": "Jag längtar till landet som icke är," ("I long for the land that is not," i.e., that does not exist).

The Night Wanderer   p. 171

This poem arises from the murder of Prime Minister Olof Palme and the trial of Christer Pettersson for the crime. (Pettersson was convicted, but the conviction was quashed on appeal, on the grounds that the evidence had been insufficient to establish guilt beyond a reasonable doubt; Pettersson was released. The Supreme Court of Sweden denied a later motion to re-try him.) The trial proceedings were broadcast on Swedish radio; some of the witnesses' statements inform certain lines in the poem. Palme's son testified that a man he saw loitering in the movie theater Palme left shortly before he was shot resembled the painting *The Night Wanderer*. Although he did not specify the artist, it is likely he was referring to a late self-portrait by the Norwegian Edvard Munch (1863–1944), *Selvportrett. Nattevandreren [Self-portrait: The Night Wanderer]* (1923–24). The painting has also been known as *Peer Gynt*. There is a black-and-white reproduction of it (illustration 115) in J. P. Hodin, *Edvard Munch* (London: Thames & Hudson, 1972; rpt. New York: Oxford University Press, undated). The painting depicts, in Hodin's words, "the artist walking sleeplessly through his house, with deep-sunk shadowy eyes…." (Oxford edition, 148). A color reproduction can be viewed at http://www.wikipaintings .org/en/edvard-munch/self-portrait-the-night-wanderer-1924

Anamorphosis   p. 175

GH: Anamorphoses, works of art in which the final form of the image can be seen in a mirror, usually a curved one. The picture as painted is distorted so that its harmony will be revealed in the curved glass. The Swedish artist Hans Hamngren has made virtuoso use of this technique.

The Voyage   p. 177

This poem refers to Baudelaire's "Le voyage." I have translated the line quoted from Baudelaire in a way that fits into Harding's poem and reflects the Swedish rendering given there. In arriving at my translation, I found Richard Howard's English version the most helpful of those I consulted. See Baudelaire: *Poems* (London: Everyman, 1993), 202.

The Flute Player   p. 178

This poem takes as its starting point a bas-relief carved in marble on one side of the so-called Ludovisi Throne, showing a young girl, nude, with legs crossed, playing the aulos. The Throne is thought to date from approximately 460 BC and was discovered in Rome in 1887. It is housed at the Museo Nazionale Romano—Palazzo Altemps.

Like Stars Half-quenched in Mists of Silver Dew   p. 180
The title is from Shelley's *Prometheus Unbound* (II:i:29).

Two of Linnaeus's Apprentices Chasing an Admiral Butterfly   p. 182
GH: The poem is based on a painting by the Danish natural scientist Seidelius, in which he and a Swedish apprentice of Linnaeus, Peter Forsskål, are chasing an Admiral butterfly. Most of Linnaeus's students died abroad on his expeditions.
The phrases translated as "amid rich beds of herbs" ("bland rika örtesänger") and "the greenwood tree" ("lundens gröna träd," literally "the grove's green trees") are from the "summer hymn" referred to in the poem, "Den blomstertid nu kommer" ("Now the Flower-time Is Coming").

Birdsong   p. 183
GH: This poem was originally called "Ornithology," with a reference to Charlie Parker, but I found out that another Swedish poet had already written a poem with that title and reference.

The Palace of King Minos   p. 193
The "Lily Prince" is the name given to a figure in one of the wall frescoes at the Palace of Knossos. GH quotes *Herakleion Museum, Illustrated Guide,* by J. A. Sakellarakis: "Fresco of the Lily Prince. This relief fresco, restored for the most part, shows a young man strolling in a garden. He wears a short 'apron' and codpiece, a necklace of lilies, and a crown of lilies and peacock feathers. He is thought to represent the Priest-King of Knossos."

Sketch (Skagen, Denmark)   p. 194
Skagen is a town in Denmark that lies just south of the extreme northern tip of the country, on the east coast. In the late nineteenth and early twentieth centuries, it was a popular place of residence for Scandinavian painters. Some of their work is exhibited at museums in the town.

The Golden Helmet   p. 195
Rembrandt's painting *The Oath of the Batavians,* or *Claudius Civilis,* has one sword too many, given the number of figures.

The Main Stage   p. 200
The Main Stage is the largest of the theaters housed in the building of the Royal Dramatic Theatre in Stockholm. The exterior of the building is white and ornately ornamented; thus the comparison to a cake.

The People Who Envisioned the Garden Cities   p. 202
Isaac Hirsche Grünewald (1889–1946) was a prominent Swedish painter.

The Last Summer Holiday   p. 207
The white cloud overhead suggests graduation from high school, because Swedish students in their senior year traditionally wear white caps.
"Dan Andersson country": Dan Andersson (1888–1920), a poet from Ludvika in the county of Dalecarlia (about 125 miles [200 km] northwest of Stockholm), achieved great popularity during his short life and retains it to this day.

Walk through Autumn's Beauty   p. 210
"to be no-one's sleep under so many lids": from the epitaph that Rilke wrote for himself and that appears on his gravestone. The complete text in German is: "Rose oh reiner Widerspruch, Lust / Niemandes Schlaf zu sein, unter soviel / Lidern." A widely quoted English version I have been unable to find an atrribution for reads: "Rose, oh pure contradiction, joy / of being No-one's sleep under so many / lids." I thank Rika Lesser for her help with these lines.

Parlor Music (2001)   p. 215
The entire book deals (poetically) with the life and work of the English poet and painter Dante Gabriel Rossetti (1828–1882). For Harding's comments on Rossetti, see the paragraph that begins "We gladly identify with the greatness of the past" in "Author's Preface to *Dikter 1965–2003* [Poems 1965–2003]," p. 30.
The first section of *Salongsstycken* [Parlor Music], "Beata Beatrix," which opens with a black-and-white reproduction of Rossetti's 1863 painting of that name, focuses on Rossetti's relationship with Elizabeth Siddal, whom he lived with for many years before marrying her in 1860. She worked at first as a model for Rossetti's friend, the painter John Everett Millais, who in order to paint her as Ophelia made her lie, covered in flowers, in a poorly heated bath (she almost died as a result). In 1862 she bore Rossetti a stillborn child. GH: "In despair over this and over her husband's lack of interest, she took her life. After her death Rossetti painted her as Beatrice."
The second section, "Museum," presents Rossetti's life; it consists of a photograph of Rossetti with John Ruskin and William Bell Scott taken in 1863, a prose commentary on the photograph, the long poem "Museum," and a poem about Algernon Charles Swinburne that I have not included here.
The third section, "I Proserpines örtagård" (In the Garden of Proserpine), which opens with a black-and-white reproduction of Rossetti's 1874 painting *Proserpine*, takes up Rossetti's liaison with Jane Morris, the wife of his friend William Morris. GH: "Rossetti lived for a time at [the Morrises'] country place, Kelmscott Manor, probably when Jane's husband was away traveling. At least as Rossetti saw it, Jane was being suffocated in her marriage to this idealistic communist and enthusiast

for the Arctic, just as Persephone suffered in Pluto's abode in the underworld, or as Dante's Pia de' Tolomei wasted away in the marshlands of Maremma. He painted her in the roles of these two unhappy women."

As Harding remarks, only one of the poems in *Parlor Music* ("Rossetti Sleepless in the Park") quotes Rossetti's poetry, and only a few are based on his works of art. GH: "Elsewhere my imagery has drawn more inspiration from those who were literally pre-Raphaelites, such as Piero della Francesca and Andrea Mantegna."

Dante Gabriel Rossetti   p. 217
This, the opening poem of *Salongsstycken* [Parlor Music], is an acrostic on Rossetti's name.

The Doppelgangers   p. 219
One of the poems based on a work of art by Rossetti.

Larded with Sweet Flowers   p. 222
The poem's title appears in English in the Swedish book; it is from *Hamlet* 4.5.37.

The Menagerie   p. 225
There was a period after the death of Elizabeth Siddal when Rossetti shared with Swinburne a house full of exotic animals.

The Window Open to the River   p. 227
"a hill of poetry": this phrase occurs in one of Robert Graves's versions of the medieval Irish poem "The Song of Amergin" (from the Book of Leinster, approximately 1160, and later manuscripts), and again in Lawrence Ferlinghetti's poem "Autobiography," which no doubt drew on Graves.

Museum   p. 229
"His sister wrote lovely poems": Christina Rossetti (1830–1894).
The last line of the poem alludes to Rossetti's poem "A Superscription" (see my note below to "Rossetti Sleepless in the Park").

The House Where the People in This Story Were Still Living   p. 235
The house is Kelmscott Manor, a limestone manor house in the village of Kelmscott that was the country residence of William and Jane Morris. It appears in the background of Rossetti's 1871 oil portrait of Jane Morris, *Water Willows*.

The Garden of Proserpine   p. 236
One of the poems based on a work of art by Rossetti. The title is that of a poem by Swinburne.

The Daydream   p. 237
One of the poems based on a work of art by Rossetti.

The House of Life   p. 238
The poem's title appears in English in the Swedish book. *The House of Life* is the title Rossetti gave to a sequence of 101 sonnets, composed between 1847 and 1881, that eventually appeared in book form as part of *Ballads and Sonnets* (1881). In her note on "A Superscription," Margaret Frances (Sister St. Francis) Nims writes of the sequence: "The title, according to William Michael Rossetti, derives from astrology, which divides the heavens by meridian lines into twelve 'houses' or 'spheres of influence.' The first of these is frequently termed 'the house of life'" (*Representative Poetry*, Edition 3RP 3.283. http://rpo.library.utoronto.ca/poems/house-life-97-superscription).

Rossetti Sleepless in the Park   p. 241
In Part 3, stanza 1, lines 3 and 6 are from canto 7 of Dante's *Purgatorio* (lines 73 and 76). I consulted many published English translations but decided in the end to use my own versions. I am grateful to Luigi M. Bianchi and to Ole Meyer, a Danish translator of Dante, for advice about the Italian.
The first two lines of Part 3, stanza 4—"Look in my face; my name is Might-have-been; / I am also call'd No-more, Too-late, Farewell."—are from Rossetti's sonnet "A Superscription" (first published in 1869). The poem is one of the 101 sonnets in the sequence *The House of Life.*

Moment in Tibble   p. 247
Tibble ['tib-le] is the name of a village in Leksand parish.

The Wandering Shoemaker   p. 250
According to some versions of the myth, the Jew banished by Jesus to wander until his return was a Jerusalem shoemaker. In some cultures this figure is known as the Wandering Jew, in others as the Eternal Jew.

Watercolors   p. 251
"a tortoise-shell butterfly": "nässelfjäril" (in Harding's text) or "nässlafjäril," *Vanessa urticae,* known in the United Kingdom as the Common Tortoise-shell butterfly or the Small Tortoise-shell butterfly.
"Professor Hedenius from Uppsala": Ingemar Hedenius was a professor of practical philosophy at the University of Uppsala from 1947 to 1973. He was a well-known proponent of atheism and critic of religion.

Poem That Starts with a Line from Fats Waller   p. 254
The song "Blue Turning Gray over You," with lyrics by Andy Razaf (1895–1973) and music by Fats Waller (1904–43), was recorded by HMV in New York City on 11 March 1935 (posthumous copyright: 1930).

Return Visit, October   p. 256
The four lines quoted at the start of the penultimate stanza are from Alf Ahlberg, *Arthur Schopenhauer: hans liv och filosofi* [Arthur Schopenhauer: His Life and Philosophy] (Stockholm: Natur och Kultur, 1924, 2nd ed. 1960).

Triptych for Nils Kölare   p. 258
Nils Kölare (1930–2007) was a Swedish concrete painter. The first two poems in "Triptych" appear in *Det brinnande barnet* [The Burning Child], each under its own title. Harding has supplied the third poem and asked that the three pieces be grouped under the overall title.
"On Average": See Edward Hopper's *Early Sunday Morning* and Mondrian's *Broadway Boogie-woogie*. For those who can read Swedish, Kölare's essay "Solus ipse" (*Dialoger* 2002: 61) casts light on the paintings that inspired Harding's poems. The title of this poem conveys associations in Swedish that disappear in English, since the word for "average" consists of elements meaning "through" and "cut."
"Squares": The Swedish poem has the same title as Kölare's last exhibit: the English word *Squares*. The setting is the painter's favorite restaurant, Saline.

Image after Image after Image   p. 262
"a ship made of dung" GH: "An early painting by Olle Kåks shows a large dung-heap in the shape of a sailing ship made of dung, sails and all."
"He's writing his name across the whole wall." GH: "Olle made an enormous signature about ten meters long, covering a whole wall. Each letter was built up of materials he had used in different paintings. It is now in Göteborgs Konstmuseum."
"Lake Superior, a month of shimmering water." GH: "Olle Kåks and I spent a month on tour on the Great Lakes with a Floating Arts Festival. After that he painted a large painting called *Superior* or *Lake Superior.*"

1940   p. 268
Sundsvall ['sůnts-ˌväl]: the town where Gunnar Harding was born in 1940.
"the stone quarter" GH: "Like most Norrland towns, Sundsvall was once built in wood, and, like most of them, it burned in the beginning of the twentieth century. Those parts that burned down were then built up again in stone; they are now called 'stenstaden' [the stone-town]."
GH: "In a hospital room" refers to "I en sal på lasarettet," a sentimental old threepenny song about a dying little girl.

1941 (Judarn)　p. 269

Judarn ['yü-därn]: a small lake, part of a recently established nature reserve called Judarnskogen (Judarn Forest). The lake is near Bromma, the place just outside Stockholm where Harding lived for most of his life before moving into the city center in 2001.

1944 (Beckomberga)　p. 270

Beckomberga: See note to "History-painting," p. 303.

1948　p. 271

Odengatan 9 ['ü-den-ˌgät-än]. Now as then, the address of the Erica Foundation (see the note to "1949").

1949 (The Erica Foundation's Institute for Child Psychology)　p. 272

The Erica Foundation (Ericastiftelsen) still exists, though its activities may have changed somewhat. Its website says: "The Erica Foundation is an independent institute providing psychotherapy for children and adolescents, professional training at university level, and research. It is largely funded through central governmental and county council support."

1952　p. 274

Sven Hedin [sven he-'dēn] (1865–1952) was a Swedish explorer of Asia, a writer, and a geographer. His major work, *En färd genom Asien [Through Asia],* was published in 1898; his accounts of his travels were extremely popular. He was the last person to receive a Swedish knighthood (1902); in 1913 he was inducted into the Swedish Academy.

1954　p. 278

"After You've Gone": a song from 1918, with words by Henry Creamer and music by Turner Layton. The first verse: "After you've gone and left me cryin' / After you've gone there's no denyin' / You'll feel blue, you'll feel sad / You'll miss the dearest pal you've ever had."

1956　p. 279

"the clarinetist / in his solo in 'Creole Love Call' / with Duke Ellington's Orchestra." Harding is referring to Ellington's first recording of "Creole Love Call" (with Adelaide Hall singing a wordless vocal part), which was made for Victor on 26 October 1927, and on which the identity of the clarinetist is unknown. The Swedish text names Barney Bigard (1906–1980) as the clarinetist, but he did not join Duke Ellington's Orchestra until December of 1927, so Harding agreed that the English version of the poem should remove Bigard.

1957 (Metamorphoses) p. 280

"Coctilibus muris cinxisse Semiramis urbem" (Ovid, *Metamorphoses*, 4.58): literally, "Semiramis' city was surrounded by a wall of bricks." The city was Babylon. In the well-known myth, it was there that the lovers Pyramus and Thisbe communicated through a fissure in the wall between their houses. The veil torn to shreds and the tree with blood-red fruit also figure in the myth. "I'm the one playing the wall" refers to the comic re-enactment of the myth in Shakespeare's *A Midsummer Night's Dream*.

"You Are My Destiny": a song from 1958, words and music by Paul Anka.

1958 (Miss Setterdahl's Art School) p. 282

The quotation from *Doctor Zhivago* reads, in the translation by Max Hayward and Manya Harari, "More vividly than ever before he realized that art has two constant, two unending concerns: It always meditates on death and thus always creates life" (New York: Pantheon, September 1958 [revised translation], 89–90). I have chosen to translate the first two lines from the Swedish so as to reflect the rhythms in Harding's poem, but after the colon I have adopted the briefer wording of this English translation for the clarity of the opposition.

1962 (K4 in Umeå) p. 283

K4 is the designation of a Swedish military unit, formerly consisting of "dragoons" (heavily armed troops mounted on horseback), that under various names traces its origins back as far as 1660. As K8—Kungliga Norrlands dragonregemente, or Royal Norrland Dragoon Regiment—it was moved to Umeå in northern Sweden in 1901. (Norrland is the name of the northern county where Umeå is located.) In 1924 it received the designation K4. 1967 was the last year in which its troops were trained in horseback riding (http://www.k4.mil.se/). Harding served his obligatory military service with this unit. His first book, *Lokomotivet som frös fast* [The Locomotive Frozen Fast] (1967) includes a series of prose poems, "Kungliga Norrlands dragoner," that deals with this period.

Tavelsjö ['tä-vel-ˌshœ]; Täfteå ['tef-te-ˌo]

You Sleep More Deeply Than the Sea p. 284

Karin Bellman: Swedish poet and novelist, born 1965. The line Harding quotes is from her book-length poem *Mars är en lång månad* [March Is a Long Month] (Stockholm: Bonniers, 2003).

Ich weiss nicht, was soll es bedeuten p. 286

Lorelei: from German *Loreley,* a large rock on the bank of the Rhine River near Sankt Goarshausen, Germany. The rock produces an echo and is associated with the legend of a beautiful maiden who threw herself into the Rhine in despair over a faithless lover and was transformed into a siren who lured fishermen to destruction.

The Lorelei has been the subject of a number of literary works and songs. The essentials of the legend were claimed as his invention by the German writer Clemens Brentano in his novel *Godwi* (1800–02), but the story is best known through the poem "Die Lorelei" by Heinrich Heine (1797/8–1856/7; poem 1823/4/7), which was set to music by more than twenty-five composers, including Liszt (adapted from *Encyclopaedia Britannica*, 15th ed., 1997). The musical setting Harding refers to is that of Friedrich Silcher (1789–1860). The title of Harding's poem is the first line of Heine's poem; the opening of Harding's poem takes its starting point in Heine's first two lines: "Ich weiß nicht, was soll es bedeuten / Daß ich so traurig bin," (literally, "I do not know what it might mean / that I am so sad").

The quotation that forms a stanza of its own in Harding's poem is based on a line from "Canzone. At the end of his Hope," Dante Gabriel Rossetti's translation of an Italian poem that has been attributed to the Sicilian poet Jacopo da Lentino (fl. 1250). Rossetti's line is: "Sweet, sweet and long, the song the sirens know" (*The Collected Works of Dante Gabriel Rossetti*, Vol. 2, ed. William M. Rossetti [London: Ellis and Scrutton, 1886], 289).

"Glockenturm" ['glok-en-ˌtuerm]: The Swedish text uses this German word for "bell tower." The city Harding describes, where a bell tower plays "Lorelei," is Rüdesheim am Rhein.

Infectious Disease Ward, Sundsvall Hospital   p. 290

"Has Waldteufel ever tried to put into music the ethereal melancholy of hospital wards?"; "like the people Waldteufel composed for / in his charming arabesques for pirouetting skaters' blades." Émile Waldteufel (1837–1915), an Alsatian-born composer of dance music, lived in Paris, where in 1865 he was appointed court pianist to the Empress Eugénie. His family's Waldteufel Orchestra played at Napoleon III's court balls at the Tuileries and after the Franco-Prussian War at the Presidential balls at the Elysée Palace. Waldteufel's dances achieved international fame with the help of the Prince of Wales, the future King Edward VII, who encountered his work in 1874. Waldteufel wrote many pieces that enjoyed huge popularity, among them his best-known work, "Les Patineurs" (The Skaters), Op. 183, published in 1882. (Adapted from Andrew Lamb, *Skaters' Waltz: The Story of the Waldteufels* [Croydon, UK: Fullers Wood Press, 1995].)

"four Ingrid Marie apples": Ingrid Marie is a type of fall and winter red apple, originally from Denmark.

Tegnérgatan   p. 292

Tegnérgatan [teŋ-'ne(ə)r-ˌgät-än] (Tegnér Street) in central Stockholm is the street to which Harding moved on leaving Bromma in 2001. It is named for Esaias Tegnér (1782–1846), one of Sweden's best-known poets.

"security codes": codes that residents or visitors enter on number pads to open the courtyard gates or front doors of apartment and office buildings.

Rugosa Roses   p. 294

Rosa rugosa is a hardy, very thorny variety of rosebush that normally reaches five or six feet in height. It has glossy green leaves, orange hips, and large, beautiful flowers. Because it tolerates salt spray, it is often found in coastal areas. The name *rugosa* refers to the plant's deeply veined leaves, which can have a wrinkled appearance. This species was cultivated in China as early as the 900s.

Index of Titles

INDEX OF TITLES

GUNNAR HARDING

Gunnar Harding (born 1940) started as a jazz musician, studied painting in Stockholm, and made his literary debut in 1967. He has published—in addition to translations and non-fiction—seventeen volumes of poetry. He was co-editor of the prestigious Swedish literary quarterly *ARTES* and of the English-language annual *ARTES INTERNATIONAL*. In 1992 he was awarded the Bellman Prize by the Swedish Academy; 2007 saw publication of the third comprehensive selection of his poetry, covering the years 1965–2003. In 1995 he was awarded *Svenska Dagbladets* Literature Prize in recognition of his important role in Sweden's literary life since the 1960s, and in 2001 he won the prestigious Övralid Prize.

ROGER GREENWALD

Roger Greenwald grew up in New York and lives in Toronto. He has earned major awards for his poetry, including the CBC Radio / *Saturday Night* Literary Award (1994), as well as many translation awards. He has published one book of poems, *Connecting Flight,* several volumes of poetry in translation from Norwegian, Swedish, and Danish, and two novels translated from Swedish.

BLACK WIDOW PRESS

TRANSLATION SERIES

A Life of Poems, Poems of a Life
by Anna de Noailles. Trans: Norman R.
Shapiro. Introduction: Catherine Perry.

Approximate Man and Other Writings
by Tristan Tzara. Trans: Mary Ann Caws.

Art Poétique by Guillevic.
Trans: Maureen Smith.

The Big Game by Benjamin Péret.
Trans. / introduction: Marilyn Kallet.

Capital of Pain by Paul Eluard.
Trans: Mary Ann Caws, Patricia Terry, and
Nancy Kline.

Chanson Dada: Selected Poems
by Tristan Tzara.
Trans. / introduction / essay: Lee Harwood.

*Essential Poems and Writings of
Joyce Mansour: A Bilingual Anthology*
Trans. / introduction: Serge Gavronsky.

Essential Poems and Prose of Jules Laforgue
Trans. / editor: Patricia Terry.

*Essential Poems and Writings of Robert
Desnos: A Bilingual Anthology*
Edited / introduction / essay: Mary Ann Caws.

EyeSeas (Les Ziaux) by Raymond Queneau.
Trans. / introduction: Daniela Hurezanu and
Stephen Kessler.

Furor and Mystery & Other Writings
by René Char. Trans. / editors:
Mary Ann Caws and Nancy Kline.

*Guarding the Air:
Selected Poems of Gunnar Harding*
Translated and edited by Roger Greenwald.

The Inventor of Love & Other Writings
by Gherasim Luca. Trans: Julian & Laura
Semilian. Introduction: Andrei Codrescu.
Essay: Petre Răileanu.

Selected Prose and Poetry of Jules Supervielle
Edited / introduction by Nancy Kline.
Trans. Nancy Kline, Patricia Terry, and
Kathleen Micklow.

La Fontaine's Bawdy by Jean de La Fontaine.
Trans: Norman R. Shapiro.

Last Love Poems of Paul Eluard
Trans. / introduction: Marilyn Kallet.

Love, Poetry (L'amour la poésie)
by Paul Eluard. Trans. / essay: Stuart Kendall.

Poems of André Breton: A Bilingual Anthology
Trans. / essays: Jean-Pierre Cauvin and Mary
Ann Caws.

Poems of A.O. Barnabooth by Valéry Larbaud.
Trans: Ron Padgett and Bill Zavatsky.

Poems of Consummation by Vicente
Aleixandre. Trans: Stephen Kessler.

Préversities: A Jacques Prévert Sampler
Trans. / editor: Norman R. Shapiro.

The Sea and Other Poems by Guillevic.
Trans: Patricia Terry. Introduction:
Monique Chefdor.

To Speak, to Tell You? Poems by Sabine Sicaud.
Trans: Norman R. Shapiro. Introduction /
notes: Odile Ayral-Clause.

forthcoming translations

*Boris Vian Invents Boris Vian:
A Boris Vian Reader*
Edited and translated by Julia Older.

Earthlight (Claire de Terre) by André Breton.
Translated by Bill Zavatsky and Zack Rogrow
(new and revised edition)

Fables for the Modern Age by Pierre Coran.
Edited and translated by Norman R. Shapiro.
Illustrated by Olga Pastuchiv.

Pierre Reverdy: Poems Early to Late
Trans. by Mary Ann Caws and Patricia Terry.

WWW.BLACKWIDOWPRESS.COM